Songs to Come for the Salamander

Poems 2013 – 2021

MARK YOUNG

Selected and with an introduction by
THOMAS FINK

Sandy Press
& Meritage Press
California

Cover art & design by harry k stammer

ISBN: 978-1-7368160-4-2

Printed in the U.S.A.

co-published by

Sandy Press
Santa Barbara, CA 93105
https://sandy-press.com/
sandypress2021@gmail.com

&

Meritage Press
St. Helena, CA 94574
http://meritagepress.blogspot.com/
MeritagePress@gmail.com

Bandicoot Habitat

lithic typology

The Holy Sonnets unDonne

Mineral Terpsichore

The Chorus of the Sphinxes

For the Witches in Romania

Ley Lines

some more strange meteorites

the veil drops + a few *geographies*

The Waitstaff of Mar-a-Largo

bricolage

random salamanders

Circus economies

Residual sonnets

Old Rhumba

Art Informel

turning to drones

turpentine

from 1750 words

The Toast

The Sasquatch Walks Among Us

INTRODUCTION

Thomas Fink

Since the appearance of his previous 412-page *Selected Poems, Pelican* Dreaming: Poems 1959-2008 (Meritage Press, 2008), Mark Young has published 36 books, e-books, and chapbooks, including *The Codicils* (Otoliths, 2013), a 600-page tome that includes much of his work written between 2009 and 2012. My sense from looking at the entries for April and May 2021 on his blog, *Gamma Ways,* is that he posts a new poem 4 to 6 days a week; this can amount to 300 poems a year. If the present volume were a *Collected Poems 2013-2021* rather than a selection culled from this period, it would be considerably longer than *The Codicils*. Happily, Mark Young's work is consistently witty, lively, formally varied, intriguingly allusive (leading to an educable reader's frequent use of search engines), and surprising—in short, *enjoyable*—and so the guy making the selections for this volume found this a pleasurable task.

Clara B. Jones aptly asserts that "Young…is internationally recognized as a masterful poet of resistance — to injustice and to the oppressive outcomes of imposed authority…" One such "authority" is the typical "leader" who tries to use mass media in general to keep citizens docile and unquestioning. A New Zealander living in Australia, Young pays much more attention to the history of the U.S. presidency than most American citizens do. In "I was this frightened fifteen years ago. Imagine how I'm feeling now," written shortly before George W. Bush's reelection but published much later, he presents a catalogue of foreign policy decisions (by presidents who served while he was politically conscious) that were catastrophic for other regions. He identifies Jimmy Carter as the only ethical U.S. commander-in-chief. The device of having George W. Bush confuse "the words poetry & poverty" "because he had experienced neither" in "Lifestyles of the rich & famous" makes for some home truths about Bush's ideological positions and policies: "When I see poverty I run a mile…It is the aim of this Administration to do away with poetry." Few writers have as succinctly characterized Richard Nixon's (and not long after, Ronald Reagan's) ability to hoodwink the alleged "silent majority" by stigmatizing welfare and getting them to oppose their economic interests as Young in "A Line from Richard M. Nixon": "... the family/ unit may sit down/ & grieve at becoming/ corrupted by reliance// on the permanent/ handout."

In "A line from Mike Pence," Young's Pence boasts that his "cruel remarks on day-/ time talk shows" provide "a 'hand-/ some gay' option" for "bored housewives" and admits that he "do[es] civility// in heavy doses" as "a newer,/ more bright & shiny way of/ looking at animal cruelty." Young hilariously "outs" a queer ethos in the Hoosier Christian fundamentalist, and this is a reminder that he was the perfect foil to his boss's "grab 'em by the pussy" caricature of masculinity. Also, the idea that "viewers/ sometimes confuse [Pence] with/ Jerry Springer" is as insightful as it is ridiculous, since Springer *calmly* incites extremists of all sorts to reveal their inner turmoil and rage—often with explosive results—just as the former Vice President's civility, until January 6, 2021, was a prime enabler for Trump's "animal cruelty."

"A Boris Johnson Compendium," which begins "Boris Johnson was a poor student who is now regarded as one of the greatest inventors in history," consists of a few reasonably confirmable details, such as his lack of belief "in global warming," and various egregious falsehoods and basically confirms that he "is a dramatic mix of circus arts & street entertainment," far from a purveyor of statecraft. Young's Jeff Sessions, who invites "the non-believers [to] suffer hell at/ the hands of the patriarchy" and candidly admits that he and his fellow travelers "have a nihilistic hatred of liberals," punningly speaks of "the overhyped climate crisis" as "not something/ we're going to waste our energy on" ("A line from Jeff

Sessions"). In fact, I would regard climate-change denial as evidence of the ultimate gesture of nihilism.

Another example of the resistance in Young's poetry to "imposed authority," as Clara Jones puts it, is his exposure of how "captains of industry" and their minions employ mass media to induce consumers to keep stocking up on what they don't need and settling for inadequate, short-lasting versions of what they do. In "ceramic cigarettes," Young's speaker begins with a bold assertion about the undoing of collective agency through psychological means: "The natural evolution of enter- /tainment is to render you/ increasingly isolated." Here the splitting of "enter" and "tainment" emphasizes both entry, perhaps invasion, and the backing ("tain") of a mirror, the foundation of reflection. The poem ends with a typical but chilling image of "planned obsolescence": "Think of a new car. Drive/ it home from the dealer./ It's now a used car."

The title, "He / negotiates a/ forced labor contract," expresses an absurd idea: the oxymoronic "forced labor contract" is not a "contract" that can be "negotiated," because the laborer is put in a position where s/he cannot reject the terms of labor established by the oppressor. The prose-poem attached to this eerie title does not literally concern the coercion of laborers but rather, the situation of consumers seduced by what might well not be in their best interest. It consists of four unrelated prose-blocks, each of which *seems* to reflect the ability to choose either a commodity ("the chic new black Trolista sideboard from Ikea" to go with the consumer's "fabulous new flat screen TV" in the first and "the High School Musical 3 Prom Doll" in the fourth), or an activity (private piano lessons over Japanese secondary school club activities, *bukatsu*), or a self-fashioned identity/lifestyle, simultaneously "individualistic" and conformitarian ("Emo girls"). But the deliciously ridiculous language of at least three of the prose blocks suggests that something or someone has manipulated the consumer to "sign" the "contract"—even if it is a "leisure" rather than "labor" contract. For example, the speaker who salivates over the "sideboard" tells us that s/he is "trying to get away from using Ikea furniture"—but not why—yet can't.

I am not maintaining that Young's poems suggest that one should hold companies entirely responsible for manipulating consumers. It is equally possible to hold the consumers depicted culpable of greed, superficiality, narcissism, or just plain foolishness, or to conclude that both companies and consumers should change their ways of thinking and acting. In "Stuck inside of Mobile," a title that plays on Bob Dylan's song "Stuck inside of Mobile with the Memphis blues again," the speaker criticizes him/herself for "want[ing] too much, &/ often tak[ing] the same," because s/he trusts "economists" who say "this is wrong, a part// of it anyway, for/ wants are unlimited// but resources scarce." Which "part" is "wrong"? Probably the taking is the issue, because one may accept that desires keep springing up yet one can choose not to give in to many of them or practice sublimation. The blues that the speaker feels is guilt—that this "profligacy// will cause prices to rise,/ babies to starve, atolls// in the South Pacific to/ submerge" because global warming is evidence of (the world's? the universe's?) "anger at [her/his] actions."

Is the speaker exhibiting self-aggrandizement, evidence of a tyrannical superego, or rational thinking to attach so much significance to those individual choices? Does anyone really have a strong mathematical formula that can link the cause of individual consumption of, say, luxury goods over a particular period of time, with the effect of price increases, which in turn raise what used to be called "the misery index" for the global poor, or link that cause with the inability of food to reach babies due to an increase in global warming engendering weather patterns that destroy crop supplies, or link the availability of such goods, produced in ways that harm the environment, with the demands of this consumer? Or perhaps the question should be asked differently: given that negative economic, geopolitical, and ecological effects are generated by a large number of people who make these consumer decisions, how culpable should each person feel? And to what degree is corporate manipulation at fault for the manufacture of desire in its clientele? And shouldn't pressure put on big business to be environmentally responsible be a somewhat higher immediate priority than regulating consumer purchases? (Young's poem "Warzone Earth has 14 trophies that can be earned" sports the sublime line: "Exxon turns to paper towels for oil spill cleanup.")

It's to the poem's credit that it raises the issues embedded in these questions. As for the speaker, s/he is overwhelmed by the prospect of sorting out his/her implication in widespread suffering and the increasingly rapid decline of the biosphere: "I turn away,// want not to know what/ my wants might lead to." Guilt, obviously, can lead to paralysis. With luck, though, such evasions are temporary; the poem's end is not the end of the matter. Consciousness of what is awry may be a step toward getting un-"stuck inside of Mobile" and engaging in critical thought about the environment that could lead to behavioral change and ecopolitical engagement.

Can we really think about consumer culture and its sociopolitical ramifications without also pondering the impact of web technology? In his work since his previous selected poems, Mark Young often engages in "Stochastic Acts: the search string as poetry," to cite the title of his essay on the topic. In a 2018 interview with Leila Rosner and me, he declares that the idea that the Web is "narcissistic & nasty, bigoted & bullying, absurd & abusive" makes "it such a rich source of material"; thus, Young's desire "to demonstrate" that "the world's absurd" prompts him to "use the hymnal that the world sings from as [his] guidebook." Young speaks of "varietal or news channel parataxis, seeking out phrases that have the potential to create an alternate reality through their juxtaposition" ("Stochastic Acts," *The Codicils* 555). In "The Month of the Grape Harvest," part of the ongoing "Series Magritte," Young's speaker declares: "Anything can be/ connected to anything else--/ that's an underlying principle/ of hermetic semiosis." Young's longstanding fascination with the art of Magritte, a surrealist who brings out the surrealist in the poet, has much to do with the former's suggestion of an infinite web of connections, which is also a major principle of what is *not* especially hermetic but right in front of us in twenty-first century culture.

Writing in *Jacket 2* about *Pelican Dreaming*, Nicholas Manning aptly points out that, while the "exploration" of the dichotomy "between form and occasion" is "rare" in poetry, Young accomplishes a "dual assertion" of these elements, and this effect is equally evident in his work of the last twelve or so years that juxtaposes elements from the Web. While an "isolated stimulus" is "an 'occasion for a poem" by Young, "the form and procedures work and contort, strive and bend, contract and conflate, to make of this seen material something complex, truer, dark," as "a dense, formal procedurality [is] steadily cutting away their veils of preliminary experiential dross." To follow Manning's point, Young's notion of "varietal. . . parataxis" provides the occasion—elements of subject matter taken from the web—and an important aspect of form, bricolage or collagistic juxtaposition that often resists unification of a poem into a single thematic or narrative concept. Nevertheless, Young explains that even though "a news hour on TV jumps all over the place, with disparate stories," "time, region, & presenters" and "the politics of the channel" enable them to "cohere into a single entity..." Indeed, "the same news on Fox & CNN tell totally different versions of the same stories. Take lines from each broadcaster's newsnight & create separate centos."

In the case of Young's "stochastic" poetic "acts," a single text might parody (and once in a while, support) a particular consistent political or social perspective, record a messy clash of ideologies without a "referee" or "judge," or present surfaces that are so disjunctive that neither of the first two possibilities are readily readable. Frequently, the poet wants to entertain surprising, perhaps disturbing connections between events / trends that at first seem to be unrelated ; at other times, he spotlights the arbitrariness and absurdity of juxtapositions that either amount to obfuscating discontinuity or reflect how vulnerable to distraction internet users can be and are encouraged to be. The opening sentence of "Turtled Regal" beautifully mocks the fatuousness of disjunctive advertising: "4 out of 5 dentists recommend/ this WordPress.com site as/ they search the ocean for their/ one true love." Even if search engines are convenient research tools, "Portico" reminds us that mind cluttered constantly with random information might not function so smoothly: "The mind is an/ inconvenience store." And some of the most egregious manipulators essentially "announce" what their audience members feel and think: "This website feels right for you" ("A Line from Dante Alighieri"). What may be an inferno is dressed up as a paradiso.

Young worries about how Web "culture's" "continued organic evolution" is productive of "a frightening and on-going effect on humanity's cognitive & reasoning skills" (Fink and Rosner exchange). In "Look at me, I'm Talking to You," the speaker deftly articulates the danger of a Web-based simulacrum replacing what had previously been known as lived experience: "Elsewhere, here, the/ sky does not really/ exist. Is either green-/ screen backdrop from/ in front of which// actions are performed/ for transposition to/ make them real, or/ else is open space upon/ which a hologram// may be projected." Young considers the Web "a potential cash cow for those who wish to be rich, a catwalk for those wishing to be famous, a playground for dumb fucks," and he finds it symbiotic with "the world in which it exists," which "is currently a sad & sorry place" featuring "a continuous dumbing down of things."

The poems are full of catchy advertising sound-bytes that cultivate stupefaction. For example, in "Le Coup au Coeur," one of the recent Magritte poems, the generalization, "Women's power circles/ are changing the face/ of business," does not amount to an analysis of the positive effects of feminism or even an affirmation of it. This is a decoy followed by an invitation to spend money, as indicated by the next sentence: "At $220 each/ they're pricey; but now/ that stainless steel face/ can be replaced by any/ one of a smorgasbord/ of cheap inanimate/ objects...." Near the end of the poem, the idea of women's increased power is negated when the speaker confirms the persistence, despite the transformations of the digital age, of both "the/ 'everyone is a winner'/ philosophy so prevalent/ in the suburbs" and "forcing/

little girls to wear stiletto/ heels whenever they go out/ in public." And the advertiser in "Russian as a second / third language" gleefully reports: "Women who wear// glow in the dark lace lingerie love/ fun!"

Individuals advertising themselves as "product" is a key component of "Web-traffic," and some of it makes the internet a "playground" for narcissistic display, as in these lines from In "the character killed off early": "It's really/ important to let others know// what one possesses — I've/ been hiding who I am for so/ long." However, such self-promotion can also be more complicated. While "IMing Yetunde," a catalogue poem that is not imitative of an instant message but that speaks of the character in the third-person, parodies the ridiculousness, superficiality, and desperation of self-presentation on the Web, it is not exclusively a parody, because empathy for her self-limitation and external constraints is possible. Yetunde, who "sells provisions & drinks to earn a living," seems to be a Japanese woman, because "her quest is to make Sendagaya the fashionable address within Shibuya-ku" in Tokyo. Why then does she have a Yoruba moniker? She is not identified as a Nigerian living in Tokyo; doesn't she see the problem with this kind of cultural appropriation?

This woman must submit to the ranking systems of social media sites: "Yetunde is ranked No. 315 on TripAdvisor among its listed 788 virtual hostesses." Given that she vends, "provisions & drinks," it's odd that she is labeled a "hostess." What else is she hosting? Are we supposed to be impressed when we learn that she "has 213 books on Goodreads"? We don't know what kinds of books these are. Or do we gain any insight about her from the fact that "she thinks about getting a hamster &/or a tropical fish" or that her extensive examination of "photos of New York graffiti" is intended to enable her "to identify the beginnings of the paradigm shift that changed the city"? As someone who grew up in New York City and has worked there for four decades, I'd love to know what Yetunde considers "the paradigm shift," but there is no clue (much less a hyperlink) in the poem to tell us. Anyway, why does this

Tokyoite care so much about New York? Is she swayed by U.S. cultural imperialism and think there's something redemptive about it that she can't find in Tokyo?

The possibility of empathy comes through when the poem begins to wax psychological: "She was taught at an early age about the benefits of technology but learnt later that it can dismember relationships." If "technology" could mean hard-core science, such as a particle accelerator, it is more likely that it signifies the nasty world of social media and internet use in general, and this sentence sounds as though it could be written by Sherry Turkle or some other baby boomer new media scholar who is sending out warning signals to millennials and post-millennials. (The very short poem, "Conversation Piece," asks its audience to "SMS" their agreement or disagreement with the generalization, "'The Art of Conversation is dead." Perhaps the Web is the ideal place to hold such a meta-conversation, if it has "killed" or "stripped down" ordinary notions of interpersonal communication.) As the poem draws to a close, there is some sense that Yetunde is aware that she could be conducting her activities differently, she might feel trapped in her modus operandi: "Yetunde wonders what life would be like if she were red & her ambitions were not so transparent." "Red" is an overdetermined signifier: it could represent socialist or communist ideology, collective action, as opposed to Yetunde's quest for self-promotion, but it could refer to the slang, "internet-red" that conveys embarrassment rather than her unabashed, "transparent," yet not entirely defined "ambition." Or could it suggest "red-hot," a ranking of No. 1 or 2 "on TripAdvisor" based on charisma emanating from her Web presence? After so much disclosure about the externalization of the "inner" Yetunde, "IMing Yetunde" closes with a generalization about Yetunde's emotional life, then backs off by acknowledging that aspects of her inner experience must be unavailable to her audience: "She focuses upon a small portion of her emotions, then holds it up against a geographical background. What analogy comes up—what picture does she see?" Whether the "geographical background" is Tokyo, New

York, or elsewhere is open to question, as is the basis for the analogical thought processes that constitute Yetunde's self-exploration/construction.

Unlike the focus of "IMing Yetunde" on a single person, "How/ much can/ a grizzly bear" includes multiple topoi of mass media advertising. It begins by noting the simultaneity of two bits of news that may at first seem ridiculously unrelated: "Oil prices slipped on/ Friday, just in time for/ the girls' drama & gymnastics/ classes." What is unfavorable news for those who have major investments in conventional energy equities is good news for middle class parents who spend a substantial portion of their gas money driving their children to after-school activities. The next juxtaposition has a more ominous tone: "Now two of the/ three ratings agencies/ agree: the summer cruise/ season coincides with/ hurricane season." What are these "ratings agencies" rating? Are they insurance agencies mulling over actuarial statistics? Are they rating profitability of cruise lines? Do people who go on cruises consider the danger, and has anyone warned them?

The poem's next sentence conveys a set of juxtapositions in commercial culture that is just as jarring as the cruise / hurricane connection in different ways:

We
celebrate the music of
The Grateful Dead with
armed conflicts & suicide
attacks, advertise it on
Guns America creating
both novel social inter-
actions between bats
& humans & Billboard-
charting albums.

If one thinks of "Deadhead" fans and the Grateful Dead themselves, a pacifistic, non-hierarchical ethos founded on hippie values floats into the mind, even if the group popularized a macabre "bat" logo. (Ironically, the band had few "Billboard-charting albums"; their widespread appeal was due to their concert appearances.) But Young illustrates that the context of violence has "framed" the gentler contexts of the Grateful Dead. As Yusef Komunyakaa reminds us in his poem "Jungle Surrender (after Don Cooper's Painting)" in his 1988 book *Dien Cai Dau,* U.S. soldiers listened to the Dead while engaged in combat with the Viet Cong. Moreover, accounts of the tragic events of the 1969 Altamont concert suggest that the Rolling Stones hired Hell's Angels, a member of which killed a concert-goer, on the recommendation of the Grateful Dead. And, after googling "Grateful Dead" and "Guns America," I discovered that Young's assertion about this connection is entirely accurate. A commercial enterprise's cooptation of another enterprise with putatively divergent values is, after all, a common strategy. Young's "we" who "celebrate" this "music" in such problematic ways is not a collective entity that he, engaging as often does in "double-voiced discourse" (Bahktin), wishes to embrace.

The poem continues with a reference to how "the eBay/ seller community is" acting in "support/ for the Perseid meteor/ shower"—apparently through merchandise with inscribed images of the shower. This silly example of "support," the commercialization of a natural occurrence that just happens and doesn't need help, is linked with the poem's earlier treatment of the aestheticizing of violence, but the shower is not an example of malevolence or combativeness. However, this passage is directly followed by the preposterous claim that "improvised explosions" (bombs) "& aerial bombardments" are *helpful* to "eco-systems." One can imagine a web-surfer obscuring the distinction between an "improvised explosion" and the "spontaneity" of the Perseid shower.

Finally, there is an advertisement for "a male model" who is also "a/ bicycle rider," "a trail warrior" gearing up for "an endurance race" in "August." Given the earlier references to destructive human violence, the promotion of "Ian," the model and cyclist, as a "warrior" is hyperbolic and trivializing. Having taken the poem's bizarre ride to its end point, one can reflect on the title: "How/ much can/ a grizzly bear." The slashes indicate that the title, like that of "He / negotiates a/ forced labor contract," is a hay(na)ku, the tercet poetic form invented in 2003 by Eileen R. Tabios and the focal point of a poetry anthology that Young and Jean Vengua edited, but these six words gesture toward the main verb that is not present. How much can a grizzly bear eat, or weigh, or travel, or destroy? Since the poem has made various references to violence, perhaps the underlying question is to gauge the harm a bear can inflict and how to avoid it. In his interview with Leila Rosner and me, Young states that he regards "the title as part of the poem, but not necessarily as a descriptor or a place-setter which, it appears, most people expect a title to be." "Sometimes," he says, "it's just a random phrase picked in passing to use as a *boutonnière*." If so, "How/ much can/ a grizzly bear" is an especially ominous *boutonnière*.

Some readers might assume that particular, highly pessimistic generalizations in Young's poems are actually Mark Young presenting his sense of doom. The little ditty "democracy" registers the claim that "no-one// knows the/ words to" the "song" (the concept of democracy) even though "every-/ one sings" it, and "since violence is learned" tells us that "tolerance is no/ longer available, is replaced by trauma." Although nothing in the poems—not even such affirmations of aesthetic transport as "Constant Craving," which speaks of music "that acts as/ axis to steady everything around"—makes one identify the poet as a bright-eyed optimist, various moments in the work display too much respect for the complexity of cause and effect, limitations of human perception, the transience of trends, and sudden appearances of the unexpected to place sustained credence in large generalizations and foregone conclusions.

In "Le Pont d'Heraclite," Young's witty slice of historical fiction credits Magritte's surrealism with inculcating a need for tentativeness to counter preconception: "Everything flows, no-/ thing abides, eyesight/ is a lying sense, wrote/ Heraclitus long before/ he'd seen the Magritte." As for sociopolitical trends, the very randomness that causes disaster also can upset the terrible plans of human actors: "Many extraordinary offerings/ have been made that hope to/ eliminate chance/ but chance rises up anyway" ("If poison minerals, and if that tree"). In his 2006 interview with Tom Beckett, Young cites William Carlos Williams as "the poet [he goes] back to more than any other, primarily because of the structure of his work, the line & stanza breaks" (15), though poems like "Pastoral" and "Daisy Irae" suggest the influence of Williams' imagistic observation. What may make Williams' "line & stanza breaks"—also prominent in the poetry of Robert Creeley—so important to Young is the tentative, painstaking progress through each unit of syntax, enjambment that takes care with each word.

Young's poetry is entertaining because it's often so funny and imaginative, but this entertainment does not promote distraction any more than it does despair. Instead, it critiques distraction and implicitly or explicitly redirects readers to crucial foci. In the recent "She calmed down after she'd finished talking," the speaker reports "two young/ girls" singing a famous "Queen song" "dread-/ fully out of tune, as if part of// a conspiracy whose aim is to/ utilize misshapen counterpoint/ as a way of moving minds away// from – not so much the current/ pandemic but the paucity of the/ responses to it." "The paucity of the/ responses" fits the Trump administration's tragic evasions and dramatically contrasts with the actions of the leader of Young's native New Zealand.

Since the term "democracy" is used approvingly in so many contradictory ways, often to distract stakeholders from the user's actual, problematic agenda, the poem "democracy" can be read as a call for people to practice skepticism *and* to be more specific in articulating egalitarian political aims, thereby working harder to "learn" the "words" of the "song." And a report about the loss of "tolerance" in "since violence is learned" mark its hibernation, not its end, so that those who had been befuddled by "misshapen counterpoint" can start to "re-learn" tolerance and to develop individual and collective ways to reject oppressive and stultifying conditions. Instead of accepting the absurd binaries like "new lifestyle brands that we/ must either consume or else/ opt out of the fashion stream" ("Fashionable People"), they can work toward alternative possibilities—and perhaps dispose of goofy locutions like "lifestyle brands."

Writing about Wallace Stevens's verse in relation to the criticism of Theodor Adorno and others' cultural work, Paul A. Bové gets at the heart of what makes reading Mark Young's poetry a valuable experience. Bové praises poetry that "represents the secular imagination, facing and embracing the contingencies of finitude, the details of life already being lived, and the imagination's own worst threats to itself and its obligations" (132). These threats to imaginative freedom, he asserts, involve "reality's pressures to arrest imagination in a putative final arrangement" (279). Young recognizes what transpires online as both a menace to cogent imagination while tacitly acknowledging and demonstrating through his own work how utilization of the Web, as well as offline platforms, can further imaginative processes. For Bové, "*poiesis* aims at the gift of imagined alternatives pressing against the (always) unacceptable real" (278). One of Young's major gifts to his readers is to provide a glimpse of such alternatives through wild, dazzling juxtaposition of elements that comprise his poetic *bricolage*.

WORKS CITED

Bové, Paul A. *Love's Shadow*. Harvard UP, 2021.

Fink, Thomas and Leila Rosner, "Exchange with Mark Young on His Recent Poetry." *Dichtung Yammer*, 22 Mar. 2018.

Jones, Clara B. Review of *Taxanomic Drift*. *Full Stop: Reviews, Interviews, Marginalia,* 12 Nov. 2019.

Manning, Nicholas. "'Each evening he would write what had happened to him': Formality and occasionality in the poems of Mark Young." *Jacket 2*, late 2008:

Young, Mark. *The Codicils.* Otoliths, 2013.

__________ and Tom Beckett. "Mark Young interviewed by Tom Beckett." *E-X-C-H-A-N-G-E-V-A-L-U-E-S: The Second XV Interviews,* curated by Tom Beckett. Otoliths, 2007, pp. 7-26.

Asemic Colon

A line from Albert Einstein

A garden hose
is most often
more effective
& always cheaper

than myocardial
perfusion scans
in reading subtle
body energies

once we know
what it is we
are doing &
the visual short-

hand necessary
to interpret the
vagaries of water
becomes intuitive.

The Fourth D-bate

Signed any legal documents in the
last few years? Written in a notebook
or on a post-it note? Made another
metal bird feeder by cutting out
both ends of a coffee tin? Become
a Guinea Pig? The hoping-to-be-
President's focus on restricting
freedom has brought about the re-
formation of The Confederate Army
of West Tennessee to help him
communicate his message clearly
to the targeted audience that you
are part of. Join now, learn how to
be a successful stay at home mom.

Piath

It is midnight
before I
get out to do
my lunchtime

shopping. Dogs
follow me. In the
streetstall under
the peppertree

a single-engined
beggar offers
me a Piaf CD
autographed

by the singer
herself. I
buy it with no
regrets & sign

my name
immediately
below hers. The
supermarket

calls me Al. I
don't care. We
are in love,
Edif & me.

geographies: Chaopraya River

A few bold keystrokes
accidentally trip a security
alarm in the otherwise

small, quaint, tidy uni-
verse, changing the side-
men into ferocious tigers.

Prophetic literature is
laying down a perfect
Sunday boogie session.

He / negotiates a / forced labor contract

I recently got a fabulous new flat screen TV & I have been searching for the perfect place to perch it on. Nothing really struck my eye until I saw the chic new black Trollsta sideboard from Ikea. Although I am trying to get away from using Ikea furniture, I don't think I will be able to find something else I like at such a reasonable price point. I can't wait until it comes to stores in April!

My son took the option to opt out of *bukatsu,* choosing to spend the time studying the piano privately instead.

Emo girls love seeing two emo boys kiss! They find this to be very hot & sexy! Much like Emo boys, when they walk they have their head hanging down, & not looking at anybody that walks by. Emo girls are very depressed looking & they tend to be very emotional and sensitive.

So fun & fabulous. The High School Musical 3 Prom Doll is dressed in her beautiful senior prom outfit & is ready to party!

Asemic colon

The latest stand-alone
software shows clearly
the intricate designs
of invisible or 'occult'

bleeding; but, by itself,
provides sparse & in-
accurate data about
the internal state of the

patient when accessed.
Additional, traditional
medical techniques are
still required. Upholding

Frantz Fanon's dictum,
that colonoscopy doesn't
end with the coming
of independent apps.

geographies: **Muscle Shoals**

Because of its
links to wild-
life decline the
Code of the Warrior
produces high quality
bluegrass. I've been
moving across town
for the past few days,
installing high-tech filters
to recycle most of it into
chemicals that elsewhere
have been banned for
decades & making
natural history docu-
mentaries as I go
that are designed for
machines first &
humans second. I'll
live with the guilt
for years & years. It's
my equivalent of
the mushroom cloud.

the eclectic world

A line from Kim Kardashian

Matter changes its state
when energy is supplied to
it. Solids become liquids, &
liquids become those classic

black dance shoes that bars
& restaurants often say they
have so as to seem as
graceful as other places that

support female pelvic health
& bladder control through
state of the art epic experiences.
Our core area of expertise is

sputtering technology. You
do the work; but based
largely on anecdotal evidence
it seems impossible to completely

fix a prolapse with pelvic floor
exercise or repair bikes by
means of techniques less toxic
than conventional solvent-based

products whilst still including
a sense of responsibility
toward the less fortunate &
references to plasma television.

This may involve moving objects

Stepping back into the early
days of the Red Lion Hotel,
we were approached by the
local plastic sheet converter
whose ethical business aims
to provide its customers with the
opportunity to buy a recycled
Anaesthesia Trolley or a two crank
orthopedics bed. "Our shops are making a
real impact on our local communities. No posts.
No Vintage or Retro items on eBay. No Home. Just up-
holstery with a fire safety label. & an occasional speech bubble."

Knocktet

There are 68 calories in 1 slice of Sprouted Wheat Bread.

Sprouted wheat bread is an ancient food with modern-day benefits.

Modern-day benefits include a garage, & large garden grounds to the rear.

Grounds to the rear still gleam & hummingbirds flit amid the engulfing foliage.

The engulfing foliage of a giant Swiss Cheese Plant & a Madagascar Dragon Tree.

A Madagascar Dragon tree is a very hardy, hard to kill indoor plant.

Kill Indoor Plant Bugs on eHow. Get essential tips.

Essential tips that will transform your 1 slice of Sprouted Wheat Bread are available on Amazon.com.

the subway out of Tombstone

He caught the subway
out of Tombstone. It was
as she'd said, the present
is another country.
Fortunately he'd come
prepared, ice in
his jacket pocket, a
survival manual
in thirtyfive languages
counterbalancing the
imprint of his wallet
against his ass. Gun-
shots still reverberated
in his ears, but he'd
stayed on top
of it all until halfway
across the Atlantic
when his tablet dropped out,
& his heart went with it.

polo ponies

Multiple inheritance leads to a taxonomy of concepts. Lineage relates to the persistence of an entity over time. New arguments in favour of the four-dimensional ontology confirm that death & the separation of body & soul play an important role in the analysis of circadian systems.

If a meme were continually interested in "what happens next," activity must be causing change, therefore, somewhere in the brain. Even if they can think independently & move of their own accord, the claim that a thing exists, when added to our notion of a thing, does not add anything to the concept.

I've always gone along with the orthodox interpretation & used the term to refer to any cultural entity (such as a song, an idea, or a religion) that an observer might consider a replicator. The idea that our consciousness is an interlocking system of memes is reflected in the early stimulus-blocked responses that are part of a generalized fear & feeling of loss of control.

Once the roles of cause & effect are assigned to objects in interactions, people tend to overestimate the strength & importance of the causal object & underestimate that of the effect object in bringing about the outcome. This bias is termed the causal asymmetry. Eventually we will reach a point in the past where all humans can be divided into two groups. The storage assumption greatly simplifies the treatment of resource variability.

& now that the Linnean system has been largely replaced by a cladistic system in which any clade or complete branch of the evolutionary tree is given a name, & the only remaining fixed rank is genus, luck plays only a small part in discovering fossils. There are no clear ontological differences between biological individuals & developmental states.

A line from Vincent van Gogh

Large numbers of people
live in poverty. It is air
conditioned, which keeps
its large, handsomely

appointed living space com-
fortably cool. But. An absence
of optimism keeps the people
trapped. No clean water, hands

soft as silk, poor sanitary
facilities, glimmering nails
that don't chip. Welcome to
the Biggest Wiggest Hair salon,

renowned for their scientific
knowledge of why biofuel projects
increase serotonin levels in the
body & for a holistic treatment

of electricity that ensures racial
disparities still remain. Beavers were
hunted to extinction in Mozam-
bique. My libido is in the toilet.

A line from Wolfgang Amadeus Mozart

A mob molests a teenage
girl. No shockwaves ripple
across the country. But there's
major talk about expanding

college football conferences
for expanding college foot-
ball players. Genes & obesity.
Aggrieved athletes protest

the fast-food reliance we have
created. I cannot sleep. My
allergy symptoms are worse
now the goldenrod is in bloom.

I wish I could swim like dolphins

There is a song Freddie Mercury sang that I don't remember. It started "I want to break free" but those two bars are all I recall. The next two bars were a repeat of the first. What came after that was the phrase repeated but extended. I cannot remember how it went.

I am in a cycle of mental paralysis. Not a mindset but a mind rut. I cannot remember how the song went though I'm singing it now. I am not replying to emails though they continue to arrive. I cannot remember how to turn on the pc though that is where I am writing this. I want to break free. My life is two bars, repeated. I cycle between them. One serves lethe, the other leaves me be. I do not recall what I am doing here or where here is since I thought I was there already. I am missing out letters as I type. That Freddie Mercury song has nothing to do with this.

I come home from work. I do not remember who I am. Somebody winds me up & I write mechanical poems. "It will keep your hand in" a voice says somewhere. I write home & come & wonder why they don't sound the same. People send me emails but I don't reply. I don't recognise the name. They cannot be for me for I do not remember who I am. There is a song Freddy somebody sang.

There is another song by a group called Queen. I don't recall who the lead singer was, do not remember if I ever heard them. I don't recall the lines that went "If I'm not back again this time tomorrow / carry on, carry on as if nothing really matters."

I cannot remember who I am. I cannot remember how to write. I write to nobody any more so does it really matter if I write or not. For myself, to myself. To anybody, to nobody. Nobody writes to me & when they do I do not answer. Wind me up / I right mechanical poems. Prick me, do I not bleed? I cannot remember.

Hotus Potus

A line from John Quincy Adams

I have a serious
question. Actually,
two. With a nod
to really obscure

Italian cinema.
How can some-
one who has
seen ghosts &

vampires feel
so comfortable
in immediately
dismissing the

possibility of,
say, zombies? &.
What kind of
idiot goes into

battle in search
of monsters to des-
troy with half his
team left behind?

A line from Zachary Taylor

People's perception of car
brands dictates resale
values. The dictates of
religion mean that no-

thing is remaindered, &
if you're young & gay
& Jewish then you won't be
staying long in Wisconsin.

A line from Abraham Lincoln

Kabbalists knew what was
at stake. Not only were
the pleasant groves de-
stroyed but names were

silently guillotined from
the electoral list. Soon, if
folks don't interfere with
anything, British American

Tobacco will be free to pro-
mote the decapitation scene
that the Bloggernacle has
been buzzing about for

several days. Just one small
problem for them. GoDaddy
recently upgraded apache
& now their site is often not

accessible. Never mind. Seems
like the time has come for
America to adopt a proactive
energy policy so Miley Cyrus

can continue to be cool. Some-
times all you need are
approximate values loosely
based on contemporary culture.

A line from Andrew Johnson

I put the phone down. Another
scam. Interactions that were once
never part of an American culture
predicated on the record chart, the

radio, the talking picture, book clubs,
spectator sports. Now has become
something of a randomized placebo-
controlled trial of a multi-component

combination pill. I have just said good-
bye to my grandparents. They insist
upon frugality. I learnt it from them.
I sit at the table with my ball cap on.

A line from Warren G. Harding

Against. My grandmother is
dying, & is likely to pass during
Burning Man. For. She decided to
test out Siri on my iPad, & that

was after Twitter had hijacked my
mind. You'd think there must be
a book that tells all about how to
self-correct. Isn't. So. Give me my

goddamn stimulus package before
I go ape shit. That wedding ring
sure put a damper on all my plans.
I'm really gonna miss my babies.

A line from John F. Kennedy

Any undesirable trending
from the marketing of beer
brands is destined to be
swept aside by the improper

use of statistics. That's the new
paradigm, a different texture
from the rest of the beach, an
initiative that has much in

common with modern French
philosophy but is a long way
from the traditional biases that
set the mood of this nation.

A line from Richard M. Nixon

In professions where
turmoil over nuclear
waste storage exists
& rival classes jockey

for power, the family
unit may sit down
& grieve at becoming
corrupted by reliance

on the permanent
handout. It's a time
in their lives when
they need ritual the

most; but in this
society there are few
rituals, apart from
the shoving of over-

priced faux ice cream
up one's asshole, & the
occasional long walk
in the winter woods.

A line from Barack Obama

Voices howl outside of
the realm of rational
thought. Special interests
run wild, grocery aisles

fill up. OMG Janiel, I
LOVE the patterns on your
fabrics! Hatchery-reared
forms of similar species

have been successfully trans-
planted, so why not grab a
card & Instagram what just
might be the winning ticket.

A small compendium of bats

The Common Pipistrelle

The O'Higgins, a branch
of the O'Neill, one of the
great hereditary families
of Poets in Gaelic Ireland,
now present themselves as
being at the cutting edge of
kitchen design, prepared to
disrupt their lives in order

to achieve an understanding
of Modernity, that circumstance
of being 'modern' which, they
say, is absolutely central to their
sense of collective identity. Sounds
like they've got a tour coming up.

The Natterer's Bat

A laptop
containing a
complex array
of handsome
graphics that
specify how

American nu-
clear weapons
would be used
in the event
of dark circles
appearing

under the eyes
was lost by
a government
agency
& now
litigation lawyers

suggest you
may be eligible
for big savings
on blood-
shed &
mayhem.

Daubenton's Bat

Now that he has
reinforced Democracy
by forming an import
safety panel to report
on the presence or
otherwise of anti-
freeze in bicycle seat

assemblies, President Putin
is enjoying a vacation &
premium ethiopian coffee
at a european style
café & event facility in
picturesque East Kazakhstan
& appearing on the local

version of *The Price is Right*
where he is having difficulty
deciding which is the less
expensive, a talking instant
ear thermometer or Barry
White tracks available
on Rhapsody for free.

The Greater Mouse-eared Bat

Bathe safely without unnecessary bending & reaching.
Reject jet air travel & embrace surface transportation.
Leave a lighter footprint on the planet. The most
pleasing sounds to the ear are when you lose your
marbles in zero gravity. People all over the world
expect a button to stand still when they click on it.
I'm going to work in the Italian embassy in Hanoi.
I can't believe Nana didn't get into Singapore Idol!!!

Inland Forest Bat

Because of its
cognitive style &
incandescent light
every tonne of
scrap metal
you clean up
from a public
place can work as

a wardrobe staple
in the same way
that built-in lumbar
supports will
retool your internal
guidance system.

Bandicoot habitat

WWAD?

for Nicholas Manning

Suppose tomorrow
I wake up & find
that, in the street,
there are fireworks &
dancing but, overnight,
I have lost all of my
natural teeth & my
investments now have
negative carry. It's
difficult to choose the
pivot point from which
the day's trendline will
emerge. Would prefer
the celebration, but
how do I rebut the
fatalist in me? What
would Aristotle do?

ethnographic research

"The violence—whether
outright or subtle—that women
experience in their day-to-day lives
needs to take precedence over hurt feelings."

Life as it must have been before the
invention of the light bulb—not
necessarily progressive;
certainly not predictable—was
relatively slow & dignified.

"A significant moment for all historians
of late nineteenth-century science."

Such a harsh environment today.

th2]

: over one million books
find it : hard to move
: on to the next task.

Vacation photos help.

What eats at you is :
that there is : tragedy.

: inconsequential details :
   :
: encourage crime.

Warzone Earth has 14 trophies that can be earned

de-
fining themselves & subverting
the stereotypes :

the
more animated & pro-
tracted the discussion :

/ characterized by
&
formed with /
:
Exxon turns to paper towels for oil spill clean-up :
A production company creating quality moving images :
Scan takes a close look at your baby & your uterus :
Disappointment, & disgrace, & calamity were the only fruits.

What is the logic, if any?
: it was a fairly straightforward interface :
: must have lived on an island.

A few days ago I created some new music_
a big jump from the old garage band
_you can imagine how excited I was.

a complete anomaly
a concentration of
supports all :

I shot a nice bull moose last year & am considering varnishing
the antlers_

A perfect adamantine body

The bladder of the pig is
thin walled thanks to global
warming. All incubations are
identical—portions of the DNA
ladder split lengthwise down
the middle. Note the broad
waist, equal sized wings, the
beaded antennae, the one of
a kind adjustable anklets made
with freshwater pearls. In a
largely agrarian peasant society
the best workers become
supervisors, are treated with
petrochemicals to inhibit mildew,
then move into the middle class.

Bandicoot habitat

Reconnect the landscape.
To submit news of your
wedding to The New York
Times, please follow the
instructions. Submissions
will be edited & fact-
checked depending on their
location &/or demographics.
FBI special agents will be
permitted to install wiretaps
at their own discretion. They
can curate any article, no
matter what its relevance.

lithic typology

Portico

The mind is an
inconvenience
store. Milk, tam-
pons, catfood at
inflated prices,
a cornucopia of
munchie-assuagers.
But the things you

really want not
there, unless a
microwaved day-
old sausage roll
manages to some-
how meet the
inspiration
search criteria.

Editorial

Fresh poems are
fresh meat for the
locusts. They eat all
the words, leave only
punctuation. So. You
write another. Then an-
other. Eventually one
will come along that
is indigestible to
insects, fit for a
human palate.

Stardust

My first
encounter with
William Carlos Williams

was not through
a red wheel barrow
or climbing over his

fence to knock off
the plums in
his icebox

but buying
a record called
Poetry & Jazz

where the second
part of the title
was what drew

me in & on which
in addition to
readings of Whalen

& Ferlinghetti poems
was Hoagy Carmichael
reciting in a voice

that seemed to me
just right
for the occasion

Young Sycamore
& *Tract*. Thus we
come across

those things that
we were
meant to find.

$E=mc^2$

Weight. Not from
the mass of the
object but from its
energy. What it
gives off, what

it brings to the
party. Nijinksy leaps
& makes the air
his stage. Einstein
is in the audience.

Winch is it?

Hat turned up
against the
weather or was it
heat turned up
against the
winter or was it
heathens turning
up to support
the sinner or
was it the search
& rescue heli-
copter finally
turning up to
winch me out of
this otherwise in-
escapable mess I've
found myself in.

A littoral translation

As if
frozen, that
moment when the
river is / between
the tides. Mud
meters out from
the mangroves. The
rocks exposed. A single
pelican near the other
bank, reluctant to
move, to relieve
the surface tension.

Chan(n)el de Chirico

The atrium is
full of lust but
otherwise is over-
flowing. Trains
leave beyond the
hour when the third
hand of the engineer
comes sweeping
down to identify
a sequential value
to the prizes. Order.
Or a musical sweet.
Try treat. Or suite.
Or segue into sequins
with a secondhand
train that sweeps
across the piazza
& takes the money
with three items still
left open. Cannot
see the fingers on the
keys, but the thumbs
are murdererous.

Meanwhile, here is the news from white-wing Amerika.

Approving a petition from the small but extremely influential town of Borg Assimilatus, the High Court has agreed that a restraining order should be issued to prevent the dissemination of any allusion requiring more than five nanoseconds to comprehend. A decision as to whether a temporary injunction against similes should be made permanent is expected within the week but the apprehended violence order placed on metaphors has been extended for another six months. Proper nouns apart from those with a geographical intent are now prohibited. The artist formerly known as (peace symbol) is expected to sue for damages. Verbs have become less tense since a curfew for adverbs was announced. Ampersands are banned since they might be seen as a pictograph of a person performing oral sex upon themselves. The effects of pheromones are under investigation by the body formerly known as the IOC anti-doping commission. Tonight's weather report will not be given. There were far too many isobaric highs to meet the guidelines. As part of an on-going commitment to education month this station's closing inspirational message was to have been brought to you by the letter Q; but acting on legal advice that any letter presenting a protuberance could be classified as public obscenity it will now be sponsored by those wonderful people who gave you Iraq and the no to same sex marriage travelling medicine and minstrel show.

languish

How do you go about creating a language?

Do you start with the I, make it egocentric? Or do you create conjuncted verbs, so that the person is secondary, the action paramount? Do you generate a list of what's about you, name them, add the sensual verbs & create additional adjectives? Do you apply some sort of Grimm's Law, d to th, that sort of thing, so the language is an extension of what currently exists?

Is there a purpose, a reason, for a new language? It also presupposes someone to speak it with or write in it to. Someone who wants to share it with you. You is now I though they are the / same person. Which brings in they, though it's really we, though it's really me broken in two. The interior. The exterior. In that case, what's the word for the entire?

Do I/you/they/we plus plurals where applicable need to be able to define concepts before beginning? Or should the conceptual be shaped by the shape of the language? Should (pronoun) — will (pronouns) exist in a new language? Will (pronoun(s)) shape the language or should the language shape itself? Will itself exist by itself?

She spoke in a way no-one had ever spoken before. Everybody listened. No-one heard.

reflections of ida lupino

for alex gildzen

The character must be
flawed. Otherwise
what interest is there?
Or else. Some aspect
of them. Flawless. Pre-
ferred. The both together.

After his eventual return to England in 1688

Selfies are the
worst, always more
than a little egocentric,
motives not always
as altruistic as they
seem. I'm quoting
Aristotle here, from
his treatise on how

photographs, slightly
altered to heighten
the dramatic effect, to
produce more pleasing
images, helped shape
a theory of evolution.

if / when

In so much as
it sometimes

has a melody
it lets us dance.

Otherwise. The
dancefloor empty.

Blue night. Words
at a dozen paces.

A dozen places
throughout the

evening. Tables.
Tableaux. Waiters

& the waiting
band. Wondering

if we will call
on them again.

Everyone's ogling this ridiculously hot policeman

Summers are traditionally
hot in St. Louis. Police dogs
die when left in patrol cars.
I've been a bad girl.

The people on the boat are
speaking in riddles, not
that there's anything
wrong with that.

Some dolphins jump up out
of the water. I dial 911
& pant heavily. With some
modification, a high-ceilinged

one-bedroom apartment can
meet everyone's needs.

Sinkhole swallows jumbo jets & more

Security camera footage
captured the terrifying
moment when an Italian
lingerie giant announced
plans to launch next-gen
battery technology &
caused a giant sinkhole
to open up & swallow

part of the Australian
shoreline, a Florida man,
Mount Everest, four
Boeing 747 jumbo jets, plus
a well-trafficked swathe
of Hollywood Boulevard.

adverse surgical events

An unclassified, vector-
based digital database
is threatening to wash away
many of Boston's historical
buildings, thus giving
a voice to the powerless
& luxurious private dining
in Bali to the rich &
famous. Chairs are
available for a small fee.
So, too, is democracy.

democracy

is a song
that every-

one sings
but no-one

knows the
words to.

caramel

Small acts of
poverty beatify the

saint. It is
the small axe

of poetry that
beautifies the sinner.

The Holy Sonnets unDonne

Thou hast made me, and shall thy work decay?

Mildly dyslexic &
made from neoprene,
she was a lawyer
who courted infamy
by using saturation
advertising to accuse a
certain mining magnate
of causing the plane
crash that killed three
members of Lynyrd
Skynyrd. It was raining.
She wasn't wearing
her seat belt. Sweet
Home Alabama indeed.

Oh my black soul! now art thou summoned

Everyone should get their
act together, create a list
of large numbers & a broad
agenda for social change.
The process can be stream-
lined, made less error prone
by squeezing the lever with
the left hand & relying on
physical principles & simple
physics. Her basement was
one of a range of venues
currently set up for human
clinical trials. Her countenance
exhibited great distress.

I am a little world made cunningly

We have ambushed the
mainstream & are now
showing the extent of dis-
similarity between any item
being considered & those already
selected. It's a dictionary of
atmosphere & ambience, this
maximum marginal relevance,
recently hauled over the coals
by the Vatican for trying to
help homebuyers circumvent
its tough new lending criteria.
It is also offering small bench-
top composting bins for sale.

If faithful souls be alike glorified

Pretty blonde teenagers will
sometimes make sandals
from cut-up truck tires using
a jig saw with a metal-cutting
blade, Shoe Goo, & a dozen
or so clamps. The Olmecs,
caught up in global issues,
sought out poisonous plants.
They were also great traders.
Spengler said of them: *We are*
witnessing the last season—
winter time—*of the Faustian*
Civilization. You may also use the
Bill Me option & pay just $17.00.

If poisonous minerals, and if that tree

The nation's refineries close
down & the mining boom
ends. The village dogs have
been penned up. Poor diet
& animals with mineral
deficiencies are bringing the
Western world to its knees.
Many extraordinary offerings
have been made that hope to
eliminate chance but chance
rises up anyway. A young
man sits flanked by a pair
of Kalashnikovs, grinning.
She tried to surf a train.

Death be not proud, though some have called thee

I am having Skype lessons
once a week & can be
contagious for up to two
weeks afterwards. Inanimate
objects will often show
symptoms when they're in
a syntactic category at their
own expense. The girl that
is teaching me infinite patience
might be Swedish but doesn't
have time to utter any extraneous
words. Instead she dances in a
language I can understand. Some
doctrines are voiced in poetry.

Why are we by all creatures waited on?

A phallus-like shape designed
especially for stimulating the
G-spot reduces stress on
the motor, creating what you
desire, the finding & discovery
of the lost gnostic gospels. She's
wearing a big black backpack.
Her reckless desire for experi-
mentation overrides any hint
of common sense—she doesn't
care if the public realizes the cor-
relation between drilling for oil
in America's premier wildlife
sanctuary & computer security.

Batter my heart, three-person'd God...

We were preparing to leave the
restaurant, already familiar with
those revelatory findings that
directly impact on the concept of
how the movements of the round
heaven would be hindered by a
square Earth. "Manifesting" is such
a buzzword these days, used inter-
changeably with "magic" to produce
a result so ardently desired. But magic
is ashes, potsherds, & bricks, three
things the earth does not corrode,
even after high rotational torque &
modern waste separation technology.

Show me, dear Christ, Thy spouse so bright and clear

A house is floating down the river.
They were swept apart. She was
lost. Swimming in a river in a dream
means either ending up in a dismal
slot at some seedy Soho club or
working for the public service. Leave
any preconceptions at the door
or doom each other by holding onto
them. Yelp is a fun & easy way to
talk about what's great & not so
great in Des Moines. Because I'm
Japanese, I never had that kind
of conversation near me. I can
clearly see a difference in my skin.

Mineral Terpsichore

Un pasajero creación

Creating a temporary disruption in the yellow trees in Canberra was hazardous despite the great distance. Economists & environmentalists haven't yet diagnosed the civil rights organization as having hypothermia. Some of the major pollution emitters say it has been treated as a child for at least a century & a half, though the new store-house of original materials remains copious & piquant. The Mongolian Secretary of State has disappeared, believed hijacked on a flight to Bali.

when incinerated

hackage documentation generation
is not reliable, will release dioxins
& other toxic chemicals into those
mainly cloud-based solutions that
empower web & mobile publishers.

Try a convenient sub-species of
humans instead. They just might be the
most economic & efficient conduit to
convey the various waste streams
usually restricted from urban landfill.

Introit

Despite the carnal desires of its Cardinals—or, perhaps, because of them—the Church does have its uses, he thought as he was ushered into an ornate anteroom & offered a chair & refreshments. His branch of the family were business people; other branches specialized in law or medicine or the maintenance of the Empire; but all, without exception, had at least one male member of the immediate family enter the Church. Occasionally they would turn away from the lifestyle they had been brought up with & join a monastery; more often they would make use of their privilege to rise rapidly through the ecclesiastical ranks. Just as the person he had come to see had done.

Early on he had decided the Church wasn't for him, but he had seen the doors that it could open & glimpses of the rooms that lay beyond. He saw the duality of it all, that libraries of forbidden scholarship could be unlocked & learnt from, that those brought to Rome from distant lands to be converted into servants of the Church, or servants of the servants, could, as they were being taught their new languages of Latin & Italian, also teach the teacher the language of the old. That the customs & beliefs of their old land, as they were being stripped away from the individual, could be passed on to another individual who wanted to know more about them.

So he gave due deference to his elders, &, in return, was given such tasks as language teacher or book shelver &/or cataloguer, each with its small emolument that helped pay his way along the path of study he had decided to follow. He himself was clear about the direction, but to those who employed him, he only offered up that which they wished to hear.

The Sources of . . .

In most school holidays I would stay with my Great-Aunt at her property in the upper reaches of the Rai Valley. The farmhouse contained a large number of rooms, each one — leaving aside the common living areas — dedicated to, according to my mother, a former lover.

I slept in the Theda Barr room. It was the only room whose name I was allowed to know, the only room I was allowed to enter. My Great-Aunt kept the subject of her own bedroom secret, but glances caught when she entered or left showed the walls were decorated with photographs of Igor Stravinski, some signed; hand-written music scores; a few fading posters from Diaghilev's *Ballets Russes.*

Persistence & the slyness of youth lead me to where the keys were hidden. So, every Wednesday, when she went off to play bridge with the ladies of the Country Women's Institute, I would sneak into the rooms.

I identified, from the range of specific ingredients within, a Eugene Ionesco room, a Lenin room, an Isadore Duncan room, a René Magritte room, & an Alice B. Toklas room. The remaining four were a mix of people, some of whom I did not recognize, but none of whom dominated to the extent it could be said that this was *their* room.

Apart from the memorabilia, every room held at least three wall-comforters, embroidered by different hands. I would copy their messages & any other texts into a notebook. Sixty years later I still have it.

Sometimes I open it at random & make poems out of the lines I find there.

The Dead Lecturer

Recombinant DNA recouped from fossil bone or insects in amber — forget it. Once gone you cannot bring them back. Extinction is absolute.

That's how he started, then stated that the fact that most things happen at a distance enables us to distance ourselves from what is really going on. Spoke of the marketplaces where endangered species are kept in cages, waiting to be sold so that a particular body part can be transformed into meal or medicine, the rest of the animal wasted.

Then came the list: bears' paws for stamina & dugong cocks for stimulated sex; the ivory of elephants; gall bladders from the arctic ox to clear the blood & for clear thought capuchin brains. Interminable.

I drifted, remembering nights spent on the tundra wrapped in furs, waiting for the mammoths. Awoke when I sensed them passing by. Found him still talking, now up to netsuke from the narwhal's tusk.

The theology of Huldrych Zwingli

Senator Sanders has an online
cadre of young men. When you

put something on the internet, it's
like pissing in a pool. I'm having

the brazilian butt lift surgery, not a
clip on one, so it will be harder to

remove. It involves taking skin from
parts of the scalp. Also letting you

know I'm getting laser eye surgery
today. This is not a matter of theo-

logical debate & disagreement—it's
simply that I'm having a mid-life

crisis & need to do some rearranging.
Many keyboard warriors are NOT

impressed. "Did you see her belly
button?" a woman is heard asking,

followed by the sound of laughter.
I look forward to the professor

tearing her a new one. For the Mal-
aysian band, see Disagree (band).

Identity management & access control

The premise of the
blues, & of improvisational
music in general, is that

there is a simple comprehensive
idea by which each company's
aspiring social entrepreneurs

display & bridge existent
interstices under the category
of Household Products.

A Boris Johnson compendium

Boris Johnson was a poor student who is now regarded as one of the greatest inventors in history.

Boris Johnson came to fame as a child star on the Disney Channel's *Hannah Montana.*

Boris Johnson spent twenty years in South Africa working to fight discrimination, then returned to challenge the philosophy of nonviolence & interracial alliances.

A drumming Argentine woman wearing a Boris Johnson t-shirt says: "We've considered Boris a fifth band member for a long time now."

Boris Johnson is a dramatic mix of circus arts & street entertainment.

Boris Johnson is noted for his long-running role as Homer Simpson on the animated television series *The Simpsons.*

Fresh from his success at the Oscars, Boris Johnson has agreed to make legendary director Martin Scorsese's dreams of having the 3rd best band on Weller Street come true.

Given all his other achievements, it's easy to overlook the times Boris Johnson was the number one side in world rugby.

Boris Johnson believes that all human behavior is motivated by unconscious forces.

Boris Johnson does not believe in global warming; considers, rather, that the earth may be heading for a "mini Ice Age." Polar bears do not know whether to laugh or cry.

bse

verb
is a
noun

numbers
is
letters

palindrome
is not a
palindrome

silent

word

she reads clocks in longhand

She did everything she could
to deny the truth, likened it
to learning cursive. Then

other things aligned, & she
accepted her son was destined
to become her daughter.

sun block

the only
poem on the
page is

not the
only poem
on the page

flintlock

When the
desired
answers

were not
forthcoming
the questions

were taken
outside
& shot.

Getting ready for the World Cup

The man relies on
magnetic resonance to
support his weight.

A nurse takes the cane
from his hands. The
meniscus on his left knee

gives out. It reduces by
half the number of people
in the world earning

less than a dollar a day.

The Chorus of the Sphinxes

The Month of the Grape Harvest

starts off with redundancy
& a table of mnemonic
devices. Anything can be
connected to anything else—
that's an underlying principle
of hermetic semiosis. Any-
thing can be connected; so,
the month finishes with
an occluded view as the
window is hermetically
sealed by an active blockade
of passive lookalikes who
render the shutters redundant.

The Marches of Summer

Cubes float. There are
parts of several torsos
piled one upon another
so they do not float
away. It is daytime.
The light comes from
inside the room. The
sky is / not the sky. Do

the clouds pass through
the cubes or vice versa?
No depth. Some *trompe-
l'œil*. Much grammar but
overall ungrammatical . . .
& the war inevitable.

Le Coup au coeur

Women's power circles
are changing the face
of business. At $220
they're pricey; but now
that stainless steel face
can be replaced by any
one of a smorgasbord
of cheap inanimate
objects, whilst a QR code
reveals a previously un-
seen poster for the up-
coming Batman film.

Some things fall by
the wayside as our daily
lives become more &
more digital, but not the
"everyone is a winner"
philosophy so prevalent
in the suburbs or forcing
little girls to wear stiletto
heels whenever they go out
in public. If seeing the pink
of the rose is an illusion,
what's illusory about it?

Night in Pisa

Close by the un-
edifying surface
images of under-
ground bombing
I come across the
Martha Graham
Company dancing
Stravinsky's *Le*
Sacre du Printemps
& stay with that.
This is not denial
but a necessary

maintenance
of balance.

Pandora's Box

The rose waits beside the
man. Or. Maybe moves
beside him if the man is
walking across the bridge.
Twilight. The man is
wrong. The street lamps

are on. Or. Perhaps the city
is on fire & the lamps are
off. The rose is white. The
man is wrong. No matter
which brother. If Prometheus /
brought fire. Now waits to

see how his gift is taken. The
lamps are off. The man is
wrong. If the other / brother,
Pandora's husband. Her
beauty given to him. A jar.
The lid ajar. The gift is

mothbite, fresh horror re-
leased, by a woman's hand.
But a second visit. The man
releases hope. & man-made
myth. Apple fallen far from
its original tree. History re-

written as his story. The man
is wrong. Is patriarchal, is
parody. Is intended to
disguise there was no evil
given by the original creator.
Gaia, the Giver of All Gifts.

La Femme Cachée

In the last pages
of Breton's *Nadja*
he has moved on
from the eponymous
subject & is ad- & un-
dressing another, un-

named, woman who
has "taken his heart."
To him a replaceable
object. Idealized but
essentially unnoticed.
Hidden, in forest or not.

Le Pont d'Heraclite

Everything flows, no-
thing abides, eyesight
is a lying sense, wrote
Heraclitus long before
he'd seen the Magritte.

So, is this a painting of
an optical llusion, or an
example of the chemical
process known as sublim-
ation? A pipedream that

the bridge is incomplete,
or a solid transformed to
the vapor state without
ever passing through the
liquid? Doesn't seem to

worry Heraclitus either
way. Couples are things
whole & not whole, what
is drawn together & what is
drawn asunder, he posits.

Then, more in keeping with
the theme, he notes that
much water has passed
under the bridge & just hap-
pened to rub half of it away.

Fashionable People

Autumn is a tricky time.
Fashionistas get ready to
face the cold winter months
but try not to completely let
go of their summer styles.
Judgey blondes, with little
to qualify them beyond
starpower, must practise

soothsaying &/or augury
in order to keep coming
out of the woodwork with
new lifestyle brands that we
must either consume or else
opt out of the fashion stream.

The Chamber of the Barley

It's a natural cycle. The
bird waits for the snow
to melt, for the water to
irrigate the land, for the
grain to grow, to ripen.

Then it swoops down, to
gorge. We hide in a cave, &
wait for the bird to find its
fullness, to retreat to its peak,
replete, to wait through winter.

La Fissure

The earth opens up.
Money appears,
U.S. dollars. Some
change hands, the

rest remain in open
view, available to
anyone. A teaser?
Or a smoking gun?

What was. What
is. An open window
able to bend light
in both directions.

The Key to Dreams (1930)

The horse ≠ the door,
the clock ≠ the wind,
the jug ≠ the bird. But—
unless, of course,
something is lost in
translation—the valise =
the valise. So, open it
up, put in, in any order,

horse, door, clock, wind,
jug, & bird so that, out of
sight, they won't bother you
any more, & close. Open
the other valise & put
the first in that. Shut tight.

For the Witches in Romania

geographies: Little River Inlet

A group of actors shooting a
big-budget war movie get lost,

are forced to become either a line
of latitude which cuts through

coastal areas under a hurricane
warning or an approximate

longitudinal representation
of a Louis Vuitton outlet.

geographies: **Bobonaro**

Now that market
reform has fundamentally
changed the environment

a metadata overview
of existing literature
is an important element

in any strategy designed
to protect security guards
at open-access drop-in centers

from / dengue trans-
mission flowing across
untrusted networks.

geographies: Emmenbrücke

First found by Ines Pink
at indulgy.com,
this muscle tee, in
a light, breathable
fabric, with large raw cut
armholes & featuring a
Wolverine© graphic, will
allow you to reveal the
otherwise hidden possibilities
of your own self. A caution—
beware of clumsy ripoffs.
Armholes too large will
succeed only in demeaning
you with a bat-wing effect.

geographies: **Roswell**

The categories — such as
Causality, Inherence, Genus,

etc. — enumerating them &
then identifying a functional

relation between variables,
does not mean that phe-

nomena such as unicorns
& mirages are non-existent.

geographies: Timisoara

Sometimes I wonder why I create my own *Weltanschauung* when delightful news items such as the one below appear unbidden in my looking glass.

"Angry witches in Romania are
using cat excrement & dead
dogs to cast spells on the
president & government who
are forcing them to pay taxes."

Ley Lines

A line from Donald Trump

The First Emperor of Qin
sported a striking headpiece of
human flesh as a show of his
glory. Teamed it with a figure-

hugging dress that some re-
porters thought was made from
bacon or, perhaps, prosciutto.
Scaly warts covered the few

exposed portions of his body.
I have sex dreams about random
people, he said. I will build a
great wall to keep them out.

A line from Pontius Pilate

She pulled an allnighter
which did some funky &
awful stuff to her brain—
contrary to popular belief,

even positive people fall
into bad moods. How many
things could she do to set
it right? Decided, in the

end, to put a temporary
tattoo on her ankle. Her legs
looked sexier than ever. Some-
thing vaguely '80s about that.

A line from Stephen Hawking

By day, I'm an online
media buyer, grew up
with a passion & talent
for playing baseball.

On Fridays I like to shoot
pool or collect oral histories
at cocktail parties. I looked
in the toy section & saw

a sampling of narratives
drawn from doing jet
set events. Physics is
nearing its end; but I

have a similar juicer at
home that makes peanut
butter. There are things still
to prove. Looking inwards

at ourselves may influence
a child's perception of self
identity, but where are
the environmental benefits?

A line from James Taylor

An error has occurred. My
plane from Puerto Rico
got laid over in Boston.
There's no comparison at all

to Saint Louis. The men are
substandard & the women
are a joke. Dating is boring
& painful. My blood flow

decreases, my intake of bak-
ery treats goes through the
roof. Can my pet still fly on
with me as checked baggage?

A line from Dante Alighieri

A narrow stone stairway
leads down to a cave cut
into the rock. Worms are
passive creatures unless

they're part of a zombie story
set in a secluded area of the
Tasmanian rainforest. The same
stuff that cleans your toilets

or bleaches your hair travels
through to the upper nasal
& oral cavities & lights up
your next dinner party.

Lychee Lodge sits within a
dark wood. A Jungian analyst
mentors single men & women.
This website feels right for you.

A line from Stevie Wonder

A piece-of-shit car
that your granny
could drive is an
essential element

needed for crop
growth. School lets out
for the day. Right now
I'm having amnesia—

but I'm not going
to end up able only to
peddle a weight loss
program. Minds ripen.

A line from Daniel Defoe

What we have here is
flavor envy, a seemingly
endless list of people who
believe that warriors &

nobles were favored above
the common folk because
their breath was redolent
with chili &/or vanilla pods.

A line from Franz Kafka

I have parked my car & am
living in it until I'm employed
& have money. On occasion
I resort to using an empty

Gatorade bottle which can also
be deployed to give myself an
at-home lip job. Wanting to
mimic Kylie Jenner's full pout

mostly seems to affect little boys
more than little girls. Cocaine
& meth favor androgyny, mimic
the dopamine type of neuro-

transmitter. My boyfriend has a
locked door & a selection of more
than twenty popular Penguin
Random House ebooks in his

driveway. He's building a rep
for wanting to mimic Barbie's
boyfriend. At some random point
we will probably change places.

A line from Amelia Earhart

The number of people living
with HIV has increased, as has
the number of churches con-
verted into trampoline clubs.

I am aware of the hazards. Wax-
ing isn't for everyone. Everyone
is so socially sensitive. Gone are
those once important personal

x & *y* variables that informed
one's life. They now have less
effect than rubbing grape jelly
onto a robot with a broken leg.

A line from William Wordsworth

If you're not comfortable with
basic geometry, then pool is not
a simple game. The distinction
between simulating & actually

having a mind creates a problem
in the health care industry—
worked around only by including
translations in the supporting

information—but can start your
acting career in just one year. Un-
remembered acts can be overcome
by the effective use of visual aids.

A line from Yo Yo Ma

The range of bad behavior
shocked her; but a high-
handed surgeon used a chisel
to dismiss her complaints whilst

upholding those made against
her by a hierarchy of elitist men.
Perhaps only the transmission
of music will eliminate incom-

petent leaders. So, walk a fine
line. Workplace bullying in-
volves new typologies for
risk management since 38% of

the crab cakes sold as locally
sourced blue crab instead
contain imported meat.
Let the music do the work.

A line from Dashiell Hammett

First thing I do on the
plane is rip the head-
set off because it doesn't
have surround sound.

I need an optical con-
nection, roadside CCTV,
a confused biker hit by
the car in front of me,

perhaps a tweeted photo-
graph of a docile Taylor
Swift. Digital distribution
means things will work

out even though the hoops
Apple forces us to jump
through to avoid their
30% cut are outrageous.

A line from Hillary Rodham Clinton

Putting the thesis at the end
of the paragraph is an effective
way of reducing drag & wear
on the equipment needed to

conduct an inventory of the
20th century. It's a method
designed at a week-long
forestry workshop in Oregon,

where rogue trading & its
associated risks was one of
the topics discussed under
the general rubric of why re-

muneration should be related
to profit. Also discussed: since
shutting down a facility affects
the purchasing power of its staff,

does the use of an inverted triangle
mitigate the effect of nuclear
winter on the day to day oper-
ations of a nanoparticle factory.

some more strange meteorites

A Question of Doorways #1

The topiary of doorways
renders them ambiguous.

A surfeit of entrances. Few
ways out. Enter, & risk

entrapment. Otherwise?
Follow the line. It may end

in sunlight or continue on
until night captures it. There is

a difference between mazes
& labyrinths. A pattern

to one, the other full of
doors that are not closed

until you try to open them.
A passage is the space

between two doors. The space
is hope. The doors despair.

La Spezia

Sometimes the
dragonflies are lost
in the small white
blocks of sound
found in the shifting
surfaces of open
doors. Bone joined

to bone, thousands
of carbon rings in a
long chain of linear
equations. It has
an elegiac meter
& internal rhyme
though the flowers

are part of the olive
family & the seed
bolls are often used
to facilitate the entry
of any instrument
designed to eat
its own weight in

desolate modernity.
One thing leads on
to another. Trade
winds bring about
the death of logic,
the walled city
becomes a gate.

The Three Chambered Heart

Even if it was as the
specialists suggest, that
in certain intensities of
light the interplay of
particular patterns might
strobe & cause him to
black out, he would
rather pass on the

surgery than pass up
the opportunity to see
salamanders come
down to the world's
edge & drink up the
blood of the setting sun.

A patriot's tale

The granaries are choked with
fervor. Dust spills & spreads,
excludes the sky, occludes the
light. A virtual night I walk &

talk through, articulated limbs
but un-articulated fears. In some
strange manner I've become a
reluctant pedestrian on someone

else's treadmill. Have found my-
self, have found myself to be
what I am most afraid of. Un-
certain. & these are certain times.

information / relating to / man made slopes

Implicit memories need
regular maintenance work.
Retaining walls stir us up
to leave us feeling under-
whelmed. We are being

gaslighted. No warranty is
provided as to the technical
accuracy of the limited
number of items that auto-
matically trigger feelings.

Some behaviors regarded
as challenging are simply
age appropriate actions—
sharing does not come
easily to the difficult child.

Take

whatever you can
whenever you think
you can get away
with it. Don't set
a stopping point. This

is not greed but it
can be good. Is a
reference library to be
sorted later, as need
dictates, things

falling into place
because at some
previous time you
took the time to
take them in &

shape them even
slightly in your own
image, even if they
belonged to someone else
at the time of taking.

Electric Ladyland

for Sheila Murphy

The microwave beeps to tell me my origami lessons are ready.

This long weekend I'm going to the opera, *Der Ring des Nibelungen*. The clothesdrier is escorting me. It's so excited it has been leaving Babe Ruths around the house for the last two weeks. There's a pun in there somewhere, but I refuse to have a bar of it. Do you want me to whistle a few notes? See if you recognize the tune?

The pool pump calls me to have a look at a wallaby with lumpy jaw. During its idle time it practices as a veterinarian. We are writing a paper together.

In the morning the toaster brings me coffee in my favorite cup. The sun has called a stopwork meeting. The moon has called in sick.

The airconditioner claims it is out of condition but I heard it clearing its throat today.

If it's Tuesday then the washing machine is in San Francisco on its farewell tour. 45 shows in 60 days. Mick Jagger is joining it in London to do some duets. It was supposed to be a secret but the delicate rinse cycle got its knickers in a knot & couldn't keep quiet. Now everybody knows. Even Leonard Cohen.

& if it's Tuesday, therefore an even day, then the VCR is covered in alfoil. On the odd days it downloads all sorts of stuff & watches it in secret over the following 24 hours. I've learnt not to try & change its schedule but we've compromised a little. Ever since I managed to convince it that JFK was really dead. Now neither of us watches sport on Sunday.

The camera tells me I have to live in a cleaner vacuum.

Something about the chi of open apertures. I go to zoom in on it but the cordless kettle trips me in a flash. I didn't know they were on together.

Too many current affairs. I can't stand them any longer. I turn the power off at the main. The gasmeter brings me an armload of carnations.

Seven of Nine

Somehow a mariachi
band in the Botanical
Gardens. Otherwise,
okapi. Rapids redolent
with anger. Polished
wood floors. The roll
of ambivalent dice.

The Stations of Lacrosse

1. Ceremonial ritual

The videotaped be-
heading of *Sint*
holo, the horned
serpent deity, is a
generalization of
an algorithm using
a distance heuristic.
The map used was
provided by NASA.

2. An intangible regional currency

A woman lights
a fire with Reichs-
marks. Paper is
worthless, without
any intrinsic or
supportive value.
Only gold is money.

3. Few scenarios in sports rival the drama

He danced. No formality
to it, a spontaneous act,
the passage undefined

but the steps within it
with a definite rhythm
to them, excited, as if

the eye had just alighted

on the open space that
marks the exit to a maze.

4. A kind of symbolic warfare

Due to the medicinal
properties of their spring
waters, the shortest path
distances on Earth's surface
have a higher knock out ratio
than any other combat sport.

5. Befitting the spirit of combat

Jungle warfare is
archly mythic &
spiritually dramatic,
moves beyond
traditional industry
silos to coalesce
into an ecosystem
where judiciously

placed floodlights
affect the population
dynamics of both
predator & prey to
create new opport-
unities for innovation.

6. Ball-play of the Choctaw

In a hard freeze,
delicate ice formations
near the base of

dormant plants can
not be surpassed in
the use of the rifle.

7. The goal of bringing glory

Why is a game so
central to our culture
& history so absent
from our literature?

8. Those who took part did so in the role of warriors

Themselves in all their
finery, not so much
for ornament as to terrify.
Social media technologies
have rewritten the rules
of activism. The breadth,
the quality of its reach.
The addition of a wifi

timer so that the functions
of acting politically & auto-
nomously can be switched
off from a remote location.
(That information comes
from a Facebook friend.)

9. Each team consisted of about 100 to 1,000 men

Orthographic knowledge.
Masculine. What is the
sanctifying goal of physical
fitness, given that there is

no need, no practical
purpose, to completing
an assignment based around
heroism, death, & sacrifice on
behalf of a higher purpose?

Didactic illustration.
Feminine. Women have
lost their previous rights
of inheritance & the
ability to bequeath land.

10. These games lasted from sunup to sundown

The games are practice for real battles.

Seasons & bag limits for most species are similar to last year.

Shooting hours for all species are from ½ hour before sunrise until sunset unless you see a moon icon in the upper-left corner of the screen for that particular day. Simply mouse over the moon for a location map.

Click on any point on the map & then click on another point. The program will automatically draw a great circle.

11. They used a wooden ball

Great circles are the
largest circles that
can be drawn on a

sphere. On the sur-
face of a sphere there
are no straight lines.

In Onondaga the game
is called *dehuntshigwa'es* —
"men hit a rounded object."

12. The instrument they moved it with

Rumors become mythological.
Telephone numbers are
exchanged. Checks made for
all firearms purchases. It takes

a while for Mars to climb away
from the glare of sunrise. Sound
is the energy things produce
when they vibrate. The buzz

amongst librarians these days
is to become the Lost Cause's
avenging angel, to show how
Northerners had strayed from

the path of piety. The ball that
players volley back & forth
over the land imitates the sun
& the moon as they move

back & forth across the sky. Gods
may play the game, so watch
your manners. Become a fan on
Facebook. A point of contact.

13. Large enough to contain the ball

Ceremony & ritual

: another blast from the top notch
: dwarfs anything I have seen
: back in the days when
: to see which phase begins on that particular day

: indications & contraindications : clinical outcomes : complications

: my main rule is to say no to things like this
: academic networks that have little contact with other networks

: manliness & youth joined in the stress of masculinity
: things over which we have no control
: without having to rely on external factors

*

How is activism changing with the role of social media today?

: because of :
lasers in refractive surgery

broke societal boundaries & deviated from
: legacy :

: differs significantly :
in budget, dramatic scope, & imaginative sweep
: other companies will never be able to rival.

*

Words are loaded with meaning & implications :

,despair,destroy,detail,detect,develop,device,devote,diagram,
,dial,,diamond,diary,dice,diesel,diet,differ,digital,dignity,
,dilemma,dinner

: historical novels that broke with Gothic tradition.

*

Choctaw.

14. He called it la crosse

There is no agreed definition
of democracy once plague
hits the town. When Montreal
fell in 1760, a group of First
Nations people simply ceased
to exist, along with some of the
core values of Western tradition.

Pièce de pestilence

Locusts kick the front
door in just after
I've got into bed. I
jump back up, wrap
myself in a fresh
kimono, hose the snow
drifts out from under
my eyes & tongue. The
cat offers me a gun
but in deference to
the neighbors I decline.
That, & the fact I prefer
hand to hand combat
this close up. Or hand
to wing chung, perhaps.
Learn from the gladiators—
carving knife in the right,
in the left an aerosol can
of cooking oil. Learn from
the great chefs—a little
early preparation saves
a lot of later time. Soon
over. Soon on the stove.
Sautéed in a little butter.
The cat offers me oyster
sauce. I decline. I've
always been a chilli man.

The Menciad

Human nature is thick-
skinned & fleshy
but escapes predation
by taking on a
concave shape &
matching the
environment. Blocks
of information are
turned into collage or
collagen, flying cranes
unfold themselves
into the sheets of paper
they once were. Is
essentially chameleon,
but needs to be left to
learn how to conduct its
own orchestra. Other-
wise, seduced by
seduction, there will
come a point, just
before the trumpets enter,
where potential captain
changes into cabin boy.

Embolism

Not waiting for what comes
through. Making a reservation

to be present at the opening
of the next exciting episode.

Someone's life. Not even that.
Hologram. Not even. Phantasm

in the corner of the window
where the cobwebs are. What-

ever stops the afterwards
from getting through the

coating on your tongue to where
the tastebuds grow. Birds ring

the changes. Summer. Snow.

The Names

Drinking champagne, & listening
to Coltrane, & mixing with names
some of whom lay claim to know me
way back when & who I have no
knowledge of. The dog is my only
familiar. It bit me earlier today.
I have a faint curvature of bruising
on the bulb where my thumb grows

from. No incision. But the names
try to leave marks. I did not know
them then. I have just met them now.
The ones who dance with me are the
only ones I have any claim upon, the
only ones I let lay any claim on me.

clusters of titanium dioxide

What is a palliative care volunteer?
The questions of legitimacy latent in the question I shall address later.

What experience do you need to include in the Assessment responses?
Many Anglos think all Mexican women are named Maria.

How confident do you feel about your writing abilities?
This meeting has been arranged to discuss my circumstances.

Do you feel that you are treated with the respect that you should be treated with?
My primary functions are recording interview responses.

Do you know what safety gear to wear?
Regular attendance is a requirement of my position.

What trade-offs are you willing to make?
In western culture, maintaining eye contact suggests one is interested in the person.

During your pre-operational check you see the Data Plate is missing. What action would you take?
Check the offender's vital signs.

How often do you need to have someone help you when you read instructions, pamphlets, or other written material from your doctor or pharmacy?
Having an impact on the world is within the reach of most individuals.

When should you have hired a lawyer?
Once I realized that animals have feelings.

Lifestyles of the rich & famous

Because he had experienced neither, President Bush confused
the words poetry & poverty.

He said:
Many in our country do not know the pain of poetry, but we can listen to those who do.

He said:
There is no poverty in the war in Iraq.

He said:
As all of us saw on television, there is some deep, persistent poetry in this region as well.

He said:
When I see poverty I run a mile.

He said:
We have a duty to confront this poetry with bold action.

He said:
Poverty? (grins) You'll have to talk to my wife about that.

He said:
It is the aim of this Administration to do away with poetry.

A shared geography

I am a true
child of the
20th century.

Too much over-
lay to say I
grew up there

or here when
t/here is only
either entry

point or
entrepôt
for a wider

current.
Exemplar: the
Gulf Stream.

A continent
away, a different
ocean. & yet

I know a
Tallahassie
Lassie. Way

down yonder.
Key Largo.
Miami Vice.

James Lee
Burke. Jimmy
Webb. I

clean my gun
& dream of
Galveston.

Bashō condensed

```
  f

  r   p
p o o l
  g   o

      p
```

the veil drops

\+

a few *geographies*

geographies: Charlesburg

In any world in which
Conservative politics &

the profit motive dom-
inate, there will never

be a need to justify
the turning of grain storage

sites into missile silos or
nuclear waste repositories.

the end of the world arrives

she ate gazpacho
in the
gazebo

under
the gaze
of a gazelle.

the / fanciful past / of kara thrace

Now that the construction
of the Three Gorges Dam
has been completed with
minimal loss of life, the focus of
Chinese high society has turned
overwhelmingly towards
variants of Dior's classic little
black backless cocktail dress,

& is currently favoring a fashion-
forward take on Public Transport
Victoria's attitude towards
farm animals in combination
with a non-steroidal
anti-inflammatory drug.

geographies: **Walla Walla**

During those periods when
sediment accumulation inter-
fered with existing authorized
purposes, the price of wheat was
high but eventually led to the
multiple-prism dispersion theory.

geographies: **Coventry**

To fill the Cathedral
with similes & metaphors
is a never-ending quest
& much more highly skilled
than the jobs the robots
we currently have em-
ployed are able to do.

geographies: **Manteca**

Listening to Mass on
the radio does not
abrogate the obligation
to attend Mass, even when
you access past podcasts
from your favorite Pope.

The Waitstaff of Mar-a-Largo

A line from Rex W. Tillerson

I'm with the President &
his family on this. My
philosophy is to make
money out of being in office.

A line from Mike Pence

My cruel remarks on day-
time talk shows finally give
bored housewives a "hand-
some gay" option to compete

with dancing lesbians or
androgynous sluts. Viewers
sometimes confuse me with
Jerry Springer, but I do civility

in heavy doses. It's a purely
metaphorical game, a newer,
more bright & shiny way of
looking at animal cruelty.

A line from Sean Spicer

I bought a phone last
month. It gets very hot,
just like being in that
bunny suit I occasionally

got around in in my earlier
stint at the White House.
It's overheated three times
now in the past fortnight,

didn't matter what I was
doing with it at the time
or what spin I'd been in-
structed to put on what-

ever story was currently
causing us angst. Now
it's suffering through a
hormonal imbalance & is

currently playing music
from *The Sound of Music*. It's
getting so hot. My bunny
suit was so much cooler.

A line from Jeff Sessions

Let the non-believers suffer hell at
the hands of the patriarchy. We
have a nihilistic hatred of liberals.
It's a good but — for them — toxic

ideology. Life can never be what you
imagine it will be even if Neil Young
writes & sings about it. Much like
this overhyped climate crisis & claims

it cannot be addressed without fun-
damentally changing our current eco-
nomic system. That's not something
we're going to waste our energy on.

A line from Rick Perry

I recently went on national
television & pledged that I
would wait until after having
public sex before going

on national television again.
Such abstinence works if
you want to avoid constantly
making a dick of yourself.

A line from Kellyanne Conway

Pops up the problem with thinking
you've got a monoply on talking to
women from the waist down — this
one so quiet I almost missed her out.

bricolage

the angle of incidents = the angel of refraction

My second-
favourite title after
Samuel Delany's *Time*
considered as a helix
of semi-precious stones
is Janet Frame's
Scented gardens for the
blind. It is an
irony of exile
that I learnt about
the death of my
native country's most
famous contemporary author
from an American writer's
blog. Thanks, Kari,
for posting the news
sad though it was.

from: Why I am writing this poem

It is something to do with staving off boredom
It is something to do with stopping the mind from
    atrophying
It is something to do with the magpie that sits in a
    tree &, in a Tom Waits voice, tells the world
    that global warming & the use of pesticides
    are rendering her shells incapable of containing
    & carrying her young
It is something to do with the death of language.
    As I write this, the last speaker of a language
    is dying
It is something to do with how true ritual is absent
    from our lives. What we have now is the TV guide
It is something to do with the way the world is swinging
    to the Right
It is something to do with the rise of fundamentalism
    of all varieties. Messiahs should not die but be
    flooded with formaldehyde, transformed into
    mechanical entities, replicated, be placed where
    any & everyone can access them, drop a coin in
    the slot & ask a question of faith, be available
    to immediately arbitrate on questions of doctrine.
    Ambiguous answers will not be permitted
It is something to do with The Greeks The Romans will
    conquer, but then we all know the oracles were
    stoned most of the time. Oh datura, oh psilocybin
It is something to do with the fact that, after two
    barren seasons, the citrus trees have fruit on
    them. In gratitude, I have added Meyer Lansky
    to the sidebar
It is something to do with the turtles that are waiting
    for rain
It is something to do with natural disasters that
    destroy the innocent & how those guilty of
    unnatural disasters take advantage of the frontpage

focusing elsewhere & go on tv proclaiming how
humanitarian they are. Only they can't get the
words right
It is something to do with the Haliburton vultures
who do not care if death is from natural or
unnatural causes, so long as there is money in it
It is something to do with Palestinian children drowning
in the Mediterranean Sea because they never had
access to the sea before, never had the opportunity
to learn how to swim
It is something to do with the fact that Miles Davis is
still alive, living in my downstairs study, keeping
the corners of the room & my mind free of cobwebs
It is something to do

Pastoral

I walk out to
find asemic snail tracks
on the rubber mat at
the bottom of the
backdoor steps. Two
yellow butterflies
map the yard, one
serving as a center
whilst the other
circles round it.
Broken branches
pointing in all
directions. Is the wind
singular or plural?

Meanwhile, at the British Museum

It is a time-consuming process,
first delicately harvesting
the epithelials left on the
pages of the First Folio, then
culturing them in agar broth
& growth hormones so the
resultant cell-line can be used
to recreate the Bard of Avon.

Some success. Four clones so
far. One looks like Queen
Elizabeth the First, another
Christopher Marlowe. The
other two have tentatively been
identified as Lennon & McCartney.

The Color of the Earth

If the songlines are
unfamiliar, then look
to the rhythm of the
piece. The ear plays
tricks; but there are
only so many ways
the heart can beat.

Analectical Chemistry

K'ung Tzu wrote that the
scrutiny of connective tissue,
when coerced, should only be
accepted if supporting evidence
such as large marine eels living
in the mother's birth canal could
be found. It was a patriarchal
attitude, like so much of *The*

Analects. A kind of ancestor wor-
ship, extolling the Superior Man,
the fabled father of the people. Un-
fortunately for K'ung Tzu, the eels
whose presence he prized so greatly
were animists, & showed no filial
piety when they emerged one night
& conger lined up to eat him.

Watermelon Patch

In a morning
landscape in
which every
nutso bird in the
neighborhood

has come to-
gether to gather
in varietal
flocks & shout
down the other

flocks for im-
pinging upon
their territory,
the sound of
Roger Miller

proclaiming
loudly from the
house across
the road that
you can't

rollerskate in a
buffalo herd is
a reminder
that prejudice
is a standard

feature of the
landscape in
cowboy country
such as this
is hereabouts.

But the petunias look nice

Miss Petunia, a fishmonger in the most malodorous quarter of 18th-century Paris, could sniff out the subtlest smells, distinguishing that emitted by an obese ghost residing in one of the bathrooms in Luigi's Mansion from that of rodent or maggot or peach.

She would often say "It must be awful to marry one of those nubile cuties knowing that there is a time bomb ticking away in her that will at some unknown date make her bloat out into something huge & grotesque, presumably all of a sudden & without much notice."

She preferred elegant petunia & lesbian flower designs in royal blue, where the plants grew to grotesque proportions, then folded up & died before setting seeds.

When she peered into the rearview—oh the grotesque faces! Each petunia had drawn up on its stem & each was turned to face her. A small LED floodlight with rotating colors shone on them & it made the somewhat grotesque things even stranger–now a blue face, then red, & green, & yellow, & . . . & magenta. It always kept coming back to magenta.

Now, a word from our sponsor. For those rare occurrences where you may need petunias last minute, XXX Cash Loan can work to transfer urgent funds in as little as two hours.

a carnivorous epilog

I feel about vaccinations the
way a sphagnum bog feels
about hunting manuals. I've
been in something of a rut
for the past few days—star-
vation disrupts the peace;
some new temple of Death
Metal enters on a small boat;

the survivors have settled in.
But, beware. The manticore still
prowls the avenues of evening,
in its ill-fitting suits, & with a
tangerine visage highlighted by
being beneath a bad comb over.

La plumage de ma tante

To illuminate & inform
the quality of life, we've
worked very hard over
the past several years to
implement a service-
oriented approach to the

development of perimeter sites
so they can be joined to form
a cluster of reference models.
In short, this means that
unless otherwise noted
you can reproduce an

interactive proximal end
to the early filling vein
that is much more
convenient to exit. We're
looking forward to our
continued partnership.

The Aspects

1. Pistachio

razors the water-
          level. Dams
overflower. In his
military crinoline
he was the Ball
          of the bellum.

2. Cry onyx

En-
cephalon. Visible
only by
cranial detachment or
X-ray. Serious
stuff. No
J-ocularity. The eye
unable to turn
inward. Only
the inner I. A
hidden cornea
of the mind.

3. Alfoil Fresco

Phasic. Not quite
in sync. The
mask behind
the masque seen
momentarily. Dis-
placement. The replacing
of. Enough to

hand the afternoon
over to strangers,
to let play out
conspiracy theories
of his own.

day 2 of 3 away

Took with him what
he could but not all
came. Closed his eyes

to get at the pictures
in behind. Sunlight
picked at his lids like

the ibis who came at
first light, not to peck
at the fallen avocadoes

in the field in behind
but at the insects
within. Curved beaks.

Emptiness. He could
not settle in a place he
could not call his own.

A stair case

Someone has
stolen my feet &
put balloons in
their place. "His feet
seemed not to touch
the floor" is no
longer concept
but reality. I am

disconsolate. Now
Ginger Rogers has
left me for another
man. I remain
heels over head
in love with her.

seppuku

Robert Rauschenberg erased a
de Kooning nude to demonstrate

all art is transitory—except,
of course, for the resultant

Rauschenberg. In the light
of that action is self-erasure

an illusion of grandeur or an
attempt at digital re-mastering?

random salamanders

Wittgenstein to Heidegger

The hard parts
I found easy.

It was the simple
things, like

putting one foot
in front of the

other, that started
me thinking.

for Norbert Wiener

The cyber
netics
of night

in
    that
stars

advance
mechanic
    ally

    & I
can feel
them

    through
my
    flesh.

Russian as a second/third language

I have made a patch for *zombies*
on the catwalk. It is flat & matte
& chops up audio in real-time.

I want to try to make jungle. I
want a clean amen break. Reboot
is an abstract illustration of a

classic learning game, a lazy way
of not trying to call something an
obvious remake. Women who wear

glow in the dark lace lingerie love
fun! Shop the huge range online
now! My active lifestyle starts here.

fourteen lines, aka wednesday newstrip

How to get someone you love to eat healthier
Hunt for sick killers who butchered kangaroos in Lysterfield
South

World's most popular hybrid amazes automotive experts
Tiny fruit fly sours Australia's big ambitions in agriculture

Batman v Superman video makes us feel sorry for Ben Affleck
Serial rapist killed after tractor-trailer runs over him while he
is distracted by porn

Spike in global temperature fuels climate change fears
80-year-old country music singer keeps the love of country alive

Japanese Research Fleet Kills Hundreds of Pregnant Whales
Could lots of time spent on social media be tied to depression?

7-Eleven 'ethnically selected' franchisees who were lured with
cheap loans
Soon, a low-cost & efficient way to wash your clothes with
sunlight

Desperate home-buyers warned against neglecting property
checks
British girl died of multiple injuries when jumping castle blown
away

Circus economies

Assimilation

In dim light the
ubiquitous cameras
might be mistaken as
pendants or sacred
rattles by those who
are nearly blind. But
this is daylight, & the

absence of ceremonial
ornament is obvious.
Still he dances for them,
explains the symbolism
of each step, then listens
as the subtleties are washed
away by the tourguide's

translation. Occasionally
he invents outrageous
lies, describing a passage
as being passed down
from dragons or some
visitors from outer space.
The tourguide still runs

with yesterday's routine.
At night he dances for
himself alone. & for his
ancestors. Trying to re-
call the gods who left
the day after the first
tourbus arrived.

Circus economies

If there were other
entrances to the cage
of the dancing bears
I might not have to
always climb sideways
into this cannon & be
fired in an elliptical arc
towards the trapeze

while the band plays
Bring on the Clowns &
the icebergs melt nowhere
near fast enough to pro-
vide a pool sufficiently
deep to land safely in.

Where can s/he be?

In the rainy
night I listen to
Charlie Parker

playing *Lover-*
man. & inside me
the mixing-booth

of my mind over-
dubs it with
the equally raw

emotion of Billie
Holiday's vocal
version. The

result a citadel
of grief, an expo-
nential anguish.

A poem from Donald Trump

I was sitting at the
table. We had finished
dinner. We're now
having dessert. & we
had the most beautiful

piece of chocolate cake
that you've ever seen,
& President Xi was en-
joying it. & I was given
the message from the

generals that the ships
are locked & loaded,
what do you do? & we
made a determination
to do it, so the missiles

were on the way. & I
said, Mr. President, let
me explain something to
you—this was during
dessert—we've just fired

59 missiles, all of which
hit, by the way, unbeliev-
able, from, you know,
hundreds of miles away,
all of which hit. Amazing.

Natural reactions

After
long
periods
of no
rain, the
trees

lose their
leaves
no matter
what the
season. The
Military

Police
set up shop
around the
corner
from the
strip-club.

topology

The line is no
longer important.

The end of the line
is / no longer

an intersection
a traffic light
a speed bump.

We can control
our breathing.

Therefore the
end of the line

the space

between lines

is no longer
punctuation or a
place to pause

but a visual thing.

Edification
for the eye.

What you're
seeing here is
optical allusion.

Enjambment
is unemployed.

Turtled Regal

4 out of 5 dentists recommend
this WordPress.com site as
they search the ocean for their
one true love. These aren't the
horsey set that you find chasing

the foxes or making use of wall
art as a kind of firewood holder.
True, they love good habitat,
use stunning three dimensional
details & rich colors to create

fun & innovative holiday house
décor; but beneath it all they're
more susceptible to illness & dis-
ease, with some particular ailments
that they're especially prone to.

abandoned measures to seize power

Conspiracy theorists
believe a UFO linked

to a well-known mining
magnate plunged into the

nearby river, split it into
five streams, & caused

coal mines to spread across
the surrounding country.

Chiaroscuro in a cursive script

Light is de-
ception, is
shape shifter,
given to giving
            shadow
  to things that
have substance
in the dark.

*

Di-
vert the
eye. So:
          light
enters from
another
direction.

          Re-
stump the
mind.

*

It's getting difficult
to sustain the spectral
eco-system—too
many ghosts turned
into ghosts because
I've over-used them.

*

I sit

in a chair
in a room lit
only by the
lost light
of late
evening.

a gratuitous masquerade

Drones distribute mal-
ware via P2P file-
sharing networks. It's
become the preferred
vector of cyber-criminals
who now & then appear
with incendiary references
to race & ethnicity, &

hope to escape detection
by posing as a sequel
to an almost forgotten
musical, remembered
only because Julie
Andrews starred in it.

Mesaic

She used
small pieces
of colored
glass to

arrange the
future in
ordered
patterns in

order to
recognize
it when it
arrived.

The perfume of the abyss

Modern

A straight line between
those two points in
Euclidean space shows
it is a second head of

the damsel in this (white)
dress that stares out from
the backseat of her town car
at the more fully-fleshed

version of herself. The eco-
nomic crisis has hit hard.
There is falling demand
for everything from office

space to orders for time
machines. The pavement
is too costly to repair.
Her feet sink into it. Else-

where the moon is green.

La Page Blanche

Centrifugal
in that it has
a center &
words fly
in all directions.

Gravitational
in that the
words are drawn
towards the center
as they cohere.

During &
after. There
is
no such
thing
as a blank
page.

Le Sourire du Diable

Oedipus might feel intimi-
dated. A giant keyhole,
a tiny key. But that's
what happens when you
run home to Mother, no
matter whether she's
the legendary subject
of a da Vinci portrait

or the restoration of an
earlier restoration of a
heavy prog band out of
Germany, known for the
completely self-referential
songs of the female lead.

[...not only to read the text & to look at the pictures but to fill the gap between the two with meaning — that is, to produce a plausible fiction that will relate them — then the key is to the keyhole as the text is to the pictures.]

Alain Robbe-Grillet:
La Belle Captive

The Domain of Arnheim

It was Ellison who suggested they were prognostic of death.
Edgar Allan Poe: *The Domain of Arnheim*

Magritte's love for Poe is
elsewhere evidenced by
a painting titled after the
Imp of the Perverse, &
the appearance of Arthur
Gordon Pym on the mantel-
piece in *Not to be Reproduced.*

One of each of those; but
this is one of nine variants —
oil or gouache — that has
the same title, painted across
twenty eight years. Not to
mention the guest appearance
of the eagle & its nest in

several other paintings. Some
doubt about the date of this
version. I like to think was done
near the end of the artist's life.
May not be true but there are
clues. A candle to light the way,
& the way the bird is poised as

if for take-off, tearing itself out
of a landscape it does not want
anyone else's hand laid upon.

Force of Habit

The sky flies
behind a gilded
bird inside a
cage which sings
imprisoned in
an apple. *Und*
so weiter; until
one hits the wall

the painting is
fixated on. &
then the house
outside of which
the painter. No-
thing else is real.

The Revealing of the Present

The present is a house that
has only windows. A thin
roof. No rooms. The sun
is cut in half by a cloud
passing across its face, re-

calling Bunuel. Is that a
pond with flowers in it? I
walk down to pick some,
carry them inside. The past is
a finger testing &/or tasting

the light. Elsewhere a cloud
passes across the moon. The
present is a vase of flowers in-
side a house surrounded by a
garden made foggy by autumn.

(Untitled Collage, c. 1926)

Eyeballs drone across the
sky at regular intervals.
Occasionally they fall. Still
see nothing. Or, if they do,
it does not register. The

bird on wings of song has
escaped its cage, lies flat
upon a table. A 1920s
flapper thinks the cage is
an apartment block, looks

for an empty one to live in.
The sky is a sandy shade
of ambergris. It may not be a
bird. Whales swim by. They
sing. In an unknown register.

The Voice of Space

Not how I would have
preferred to spend
my time. But when The
World asks you to
take a turn around
the lawn after lunch
how can you turn
the invitation down.
Forwent the siesta ex-
pecting insight &
the exposition of an
ideal set of corporate
goals. Instead subjected
to an egotistical list
of mergers, takeovers,
strategic alliances, &
plays that have no
other purpose than
an exercise of
personal power. So sad
to find The World is
just another business
that is run by men.

Ika Loch's Bordello

Her speciality is to
assume positions in
which she holds up to
the consumer a smaller
version of herself which
holds a smaller version of
herself which holds etc. Seen
from one side it might seem
she is reducing her exposure
or possibly offering optional
extras. But Magritte quite

often shows reflections in
reverse, sees things from be-
hind as it were. Which means
instead of demeaning herself
she is actually posing this way
to gradually impose herself by
growing larger & eventually
dominate the space around. So,
no reaction from the front,
but the building at the back
is obviously excited by it all.

The Perfume of the Abyss

Incorrect to talk of the
food chain as if it were
a single entity. Absence
blots people out. Others
emerge, elements of a
sense of guilt that is
sometimes offered up
as a straight radiant,
sometimes as the center-
piece of a *vesica piscis,*
the fish's bladder favored
by some religions. The
abyss is redolent of each
& every aspect — or
would be if someone were
there to be aware of them.

The Explanation

Father is discarded, is
dying, may even be
already dead. Freud
sits at the prestige table
offering up thanks to
Sophocles, thinking
that without the help
of *Oedipus Tyrannus*
he may not have even
managed to get a seat
at the table nearest to
the kitchen. Mother
has another drink, says
to her son: "Now I have
the carrot & the stick in
one." Son: "*In vino veri-
tas*. Fuck you, Mother."

Les surprises et l'océan

There is a head shaped
like an ear that carries with-
in it a magic mirror that
may or may not hear, but
offers a diffident aspect

of the ocean. A woman in
a little black dress carries
it as she waits for dinner
to be served. The narrow
pyramids of sand are there

to snack on if she gets hung-
ry, fretting for her date to
arrive. Who may surprise her.
The sea is fairly flat, seems
perfect for galloping in on.

The Gun

An object
is not so
attached

to its
name
that another

one more
suitable
cannot

be found
to take
its place.

le terminus
œil de triton
miasme

la girafe
éternité
le tronc d'arbre

ce cavalier
campagne
philosophique

la liste
lambiner
le canon.

A vicarious life—the backing tracks

Forget the

flight of small
cheeping birds
that WCW wrote
about—old age
is a house-arrest
bracelet woven
from the stupid-
ities that you

now commit
when you venture
out, & fallible be-
cause it doesn't
always signal
an errant action.

intimidation

She left gaps
in the con-
versation
to be filled
with his guilt.

The Archer

Just as I pass over
the Tropic of
Capricorn, 100 ibis
rise & circle above
me. Egyptian birds
in the Queensland sky.
Perhaps they have been
released to celebrate

the Grand Reopening
of the famed Library
of Alexandria. Maybe
Rockhampton is to
be the new repository
of ancient wisdom &
I am getting in
on the ground floor.

Ma Caw

In the back-
ground, the
empty vessel
that is Céline
Dion parrots
the words of
others with
as much e-
motion as a
cash register
can generate.

in edifices, edification

Nobody was there
when he visited

the Great Hall
of The People.

Conversation Piece

"The art of
conversation is dead."

Do you agree or
disagree? SMS

your answer
to 1234 567 890.

chamomile terraces

The post-nuclear world
is living with its mother

in a rented sand box
that consists mainly

of a hot tub & a shaky
balcony that has some

sort of obstruction which
tends to spoil the view.

taxonomic drift

ceramic cigarettes

The natural evolution of enter-
tainment is to render you
increasingly isolated.

When global warming is
commercialized, the smart-
phone is expected to
become burdensome.

Unplug your Flat Screen TV
from the white picket fence
before you begin.

Be skeptical of politics, the police,
the furnish of fiber pulp.

Think of a new car. Drive
it home from the dealer.
It's now a used car.

9/11/2004 Things to do today (in no particular order)

Give Iraq back to the Iraqis
Give Chechnya back to the Chechens
Announce there is oil in Sudan
Start an internment camp for the world's political leaders in Novaya Zemlya
Put a sign above its entrance way (at this time E.E. Cummings' "a politician is an arse upon" seems most appropriate)
Invite George W Borg to open it
Make him the first inmate
Work out how to clone Nelson Mandela (1)
Work out how to clone Genghis Khan but keep them in reserve in case (1) doesn't work out & world peace is a myth
Ban all music except for Doris Day songs
Abolish slavery
Come ashore with my slowboat crew
Reanimate Godzilla
Tell the world all poetry is political
Practice what I preach

9/12/2004 How yesterday's "things to do list" went

Went to give Iraq back but the oil companies & Halliburton asked me to postpone my actions
Went to give Chechnya back but the oil companies asked me to postpone
Went to announce there was oil in Sudan but the oil companies asked me to postpone the announcement until after Halliburton had finished in Iraq
Invited George W Borg to open the internment camp but the oil companies & Halliburton asked me to postpone it because there was an election campaign going on that they needed to win

Asked if Dick Cheney could come instead. After all he is the real President but because of protocol I had to ask the figuredickhead first. Cheney is thinking about it
Have plans in place to change the sign over the gate if Cheney comes. Now it will be a misquoting of Allen Ginsberg. "America I've given you nothing & now I'm all."
Have cloned Nelson Mandela but found I cannot use him because Halliburton & the oil companies have a joint patent out on world peace & have locked it away in their vaults because it's bad for their current business
Have cloned Genghis Khan. Am working out how the Golden Horde can launch an assault on the above-mentioned vaults
Discovered Doris Day is not under contract to any of the oil companies or Halliburton & therefore nobody will add her to their play lists
Have gone to the Supreme Court asking for a definition of slavery because Halliburton & the oil companies claim that their employee contracts do not fall inside that purview
Couldn't get any petrol to run my slowboat. Am taking it to China for refueling
Reanimated Godzilla but discovered he was under contract to the oil companies as a source of alternative energy & to Halliburton as a demolition expert
Told the world all poetry is political. The main response was "what's poetry?" Most of the rest googled "political poetry", got *poetry that regularly speaks about political, economic & social issues of immediate interest to a wide audience, is nowhere to be found,* & decided to let others do their thinking for them
Went to write a political poem. Discovered *Click here to send a note of encouragement to Halliburton employees* & used it to write notes to George W. & Dick Cheney instead

erasmussed

In the kingdom of
the blond(e), the un-

dyed (wo)man is
considered kinky.

all of them gone

I get up & think
that maybe it's
an Irving Berlin
day. & then I
think who the
fuck these days
would know who
Irving Berlin is?
So I just go off
& do my daily
bit, singing *Blue*
Skies smiling at me
& moving further
back in time.

geographies: Anacostia

Can a semicolon be used to
join incomplete post war
nuclear families with gender-
asymmetric family roles in
the Washington DC area?

Look at Me, I'm Talking to You

Elsewhere, here, the
sky does not really
exist. Is either green-
screen backdrop from
in front of which

actions are performed
for transposition to
make them real, or
else is open space upon
which a hologram

may be projected. Form,
what there is of it, is
gained through the
curvature of the Earth,
the peripheral sight

lines of optic nerves.
No clipped images to
overlay; so, filled-up
with facts from many
imaginings—castles,

ships, a set of crystal
glasses, an eagle or
two. Words have no
place in it. She wonders
what color her eyes are.

A Poisonous Autumn

The ptarmigan cast a
gloomy half light across
the desolate fire-marked
streams. Orioles who a-
void eating the poisonous
parts of the monarch

butterfly cost nothing but
wind their way into drains
& wells just when things
start to dull in the forest.
Some of the meadow
grasses now being grazed

by a flock of sheep are alien.
The ah, released from the
sentence, flew off like a ball.
Small rodents among the rocks
fell to quoting & referring to
grand & pleasing couplets.

Today the

postman brought
me a poem
from William
Carlos Williams.

Special delivery.
No letter, no
card. The
spoken word.

Stopped his bike
at the top
of the steps &
started to recite

in a voice
equally suited
to delivering
babies or poems.

"A big young bareheaded woman
in an apron...."

I was im-
pressed.
Waited un-
til he had

finished &
gave him the
flight of small
cheeping birds

that were
in the ice

box & which
you were

probably
saving
for my
old age.

Forgive me.

don't let me be

Am temporarily

p
o
e
m
-ed
out

so switch off

& switch on

an Eric Burdon
doco
on cable tv.

Find myself
still tinglified by
The House of The Rising Sun
after all these years

but am surprised — horrified, even —by the story Eric Burdon tells of he & Jimi Hendrix looking out their hotel window in London watching an anti-Vietnam War protest & Burdon makes some remark & Hendrix replies: "just wait until the Chinese Communists come pouring down through Vietnam & take over the whole of South-East Asia & then the world."

So difficult to
reconcile the great
gypsy guitarist
of *Hey Joe*

as someone who
supported any
Domino theory
apart from Fats.

*

Am
not surprised
to find
Alan Price
talked about but
not talked
to
since
the split
in '64 or '65

when Price
went off
with Allen
Ginsberg to join
Bob Dylan's
Travellin' thru
England Medicine
& Minstrel Show
& was left forever in
a corner of some
unforeign field
being told

don't
look
back

but
came

back

later
to record
one of the
all time great tracks

I
put a
spell on you

which Nina
Simone also
recorded around
the same time.

*

The same
Nina Simone
who had earlier
recorded

Don't let me be
misunderstood

& who later
accused Burdon
of ripping off her
version of the song

& taking all
the credit for it
& making all
the money from it.

*

Though,
years after,

in one of
those acts
that under-
pin
the cyclical
& cynical
nature of both
music &
fashion

Burdon —
in concert
with his
current band —

did a version
of the song

to close
off
the
pro-
gram

that owed more

to Ms Simone
than to
The Animals
of 40 years ago.

misunderstood

A dance in five syllables, of which this is only three

Elegance is in
the eye. Either
of the beholder
or the beholden
to. Holds on to

Odessa in the
Steppes where
music is a
susurration, a
faint serration be-

fore the line goes
flat. Eyes bleed in
sepia. The line the
Steppes follow is
not the pattern

of the following
dance. Is not
a line of steps.
Elegance is. The
dance follows.

Lines writ in the week leading up to my 77th birthday

As I approach my seventy-eighth year, I decide it is time I wrote a really long poem. A *meisterarbeit* as it were, tying in together everything I have learnt over my lifetime & distilling it into an output of such insight & incisiveness that, even if I didn't finish it, there would be enough for the most obdurate of critics to proclaim it the work that showed literature the way forward into the second half of the twentyfirst century.

I might be forced to make a deal with someone. That's nothing new. Faust made a pact with the Devil, Pound with Walt Whitman. Without resorting to higher — or lower — beings there's quite a choice even if you only include those who have a few good long poems under their belt. I make a pact with you, William Carlos Williams. Or Allen Ginsberg. Or Octavio Paz.

But being vain, there'd have to be a few things before I got round to poetry. I mean, my butt has disappeared over the years; that'd have to come back. & the handfuls of fat around the belly would have to go. The eyes enlightened. A good scourge of the lungs & trachea to get rid of the tar buildup, & then a patchless cessation of my desire for nicotine. One morning wake up not to find myself metamorphosed into a giant cigarette-craving beetle. Gregor Samsa, eat your heart out.

The blood would be flowing the way it should / wouldn't it be good / to be able to crack wood. Or at least keep the tree standing upright. Because that's one of the problems with old age — your cock has a mind of its own that points in a totally different direction to the mind of its own it had fifty or sixty years ago.

So you're revitalized & ready to go, & suddenly the urge to write long poems disappears out the door because there's too much else to do. Unfortunately, the need to write doesn't join it. Now it's compromise time, but there has to be a way to retain the best of both worlds. What to do? Who else is there? Thinking time………..

I make a pact with you, Matsuo Bashō.

Patently absurd

I have copyrighted the word 'word.' From now on it must be written word©. Microsoft threatens legal action. I respond by billing them for royalties.

I have taken patents out on every example of a word©, in every language. Even the dead, even the non-verbal. The Vatican issues a Papal Bull, & then withdraws it when I point out their move away from conducting masses in Latin severely undermines their case. I do a deal with Christian Fundamentalists, by which speaking in tongues is covered by a cost-effective generic licence. I exclude all politicians everywhere since, on past performance, most of them use language improperly & tend to drive many otherwise true believers back to domains within my domain. The 'lost tribes' of Asia & South America discuss a class action but decide against it when I mention that legal jargon incurs such massive royalties that to cover them would mean handing over the rest of their rainforests which they haven't yet signed away.

I am in the process of genetically modifying word©s so they cannot be grown from rootstock, are viable for one season only. I talk about reducing all languages down to a single word©. Monsanto claims this is plagiarism. I do a deal with them.

Already I own nearly all the letters including variations on them. Vispo practitioners & calligraphers are outraged. I own most punctuation marks, & symbols down to the last ampersand. Only ™ remains in the public domain.

My intention is that word©s lose all meaning, all touch with reality. I wish to turn them into abstract commodities that are traded on the Futures Exchange or on the Money Market where barely-out-of-their-teens / already-burnt-out / ready-to-drop-out financial advisers shit their pants every time an aging Chairman of the Federal Dictionary opens his or her mouth, & then have orgasms in the ordure if the haruspices say the news is good.

I dream of the time when the current value of key word©s can be found chalked up outside a *bureau de change,* revised daily, hourly if the trading price is volatile.

No-one speaks to me anymore. No-one can afford to.

from 729 words

#4

for
of
all,

; indeed, it
an i have to

In order
for
.

. are not
acceptable
to.

Expect is

to fix is

will focus on
the closest
part of that

Followed by roughly
seventy years of
Water?

#12

a dialogue on racism
received renewed interest
to describe
—a

a longitudinal direction
composed of
—a is

from the
relative comfort

of his home
in Roswell

The purpose lies in the concept.
Extensive knowledge is important.
We must explicitly define
même si les codes ne sont pas dépassés.

The phenomenon of loss
is often observed as
counter-
point; to new information:

Residual sonnets

grand baroque

Millennials are obsessed. The
manufacturer of your grandpa's
fishing hat has been inundated
with requests to act as part-time
agents for them. In these days
when workers bounce from one
job to another, it seems like every-
one is looking for a side hustle

with a bonus 1GB thrown in. I
have another type of gig to get to,
making wristbands, differentiated
by being translated into Sanskrit,
that get you into any party focused
on the isolation of the elderly.

the narrator calls on volunteers

The basic idea is pretty simple.
Scour a newspaper morgue &
make a list of thirty five otherwise
forgotten things. How clonal grade
medium & supplement should be
stored in the dark at -20°C. How
Michelangelo forced your mother
at gunpoint to help him paint the

Sistine's ceiling. Why Apple cut
8000 jobs at Eastern Australia's
largest grains handler. That sort
of thing. Then, & only then, will
History admit to its criminal past
& be forced to transform itself.

Comments are moderated

Do not strain to see what
exists in another space—the
narrator's name is purposely
not given. A bit like soda pop
bottles discarded in a drygoods
store, people seem to harbor
opposite tendencies. We've
been listening & have taken

into consideration all of your
feedback. The dictates of religion
let us vary the way the techno-
logy we use works. Don't have a
Kindle? Well at least you've got
a mother-fuckin' job right now.

originally released in 2001

If there is a sudden power
failure controlled by hori-
zontal differences, or, failing
that, protests against the
arrest of a hardline Muslim
cleric turning violent, don't
be surprised to discover that
physics has run over your

dogma, destroying its new
airborne surveillance & control
system. With incidents like those,
how can the state guarantee a
safe supply of marijuana? The
state can't. No single entity can.

conv)ex, conc(ave

While the rest of
the civilized world
is calling for an end
to the violence occuring
around the globe, the
ordinals of The Vatican
have re-entered the closet
to come to a decision

about the association
between the intake of
fresh fruit & elective
caesarean sections, &,
also, why some dogs
only know one word.

Sect

In his first public statement
since taking an unknown
dose of organophosphate
insecticide, the King of Nepal
said that he was struck speech-
less by the notation, fingering,
& keyboard diagrams under-
lying the stylistic aspects

of the artwork of Wassily
Kandinsky. How by the
removal of one element of cDNA
they could be used as a sex-
pheromone trap to lure blood-
sucking pests to their deaths.

Esoteric criteria

What turns your crank? Revs
your engine? Gets you going?
I love—used to love—painting
glass. Then I found you could
download ebooks by Mark Young
for FREE! Including "How to con-
vert your post lantern gaslight
to electric." Realized absolute

moral privilege was flexible,
scalable, & cost effective. Now I
seek to find how much physical
activity inside a Nags Head
condo rental will appease the re-
spective bases in the primaries?

What Xero offers

The leading online storage &
file delivery service is envied
for her use of the tropes she
keeps in a secret gulag of
unique art forms. Her young
adult ministry is a global
provider of real-time product-
based symposia that encourage

our youth to buy pharmaceuticals
& pirated DVDs. All asymmetry
& angularity, she writes in an open-
access article that the feminist move-
ment didn't actually help women. She
is set to earn millions from her app.

The politics of dogs

People living in poverty are included
to protect the purity of dog bloodlines —
secularism as a political philosophy
cannot be neutral. I'm currently living
in a car in Austin, TX with my boyfriend,
functionally illiterate, importuned into
requesting that his bloodline be traced. I
lace up my trainers, head out the door,

remembering that dogs rarely feature
in serious political science research. The
newly formed Boy Scouts Association
of Romania tweets that every dog needs
to feel important, that the use of kennel
crates for humans is "animal abuse."

Old Rhumba

A Salute to James Schuyler

Never the initial
act, planting, even
if used as such, as in
"planting the seed." Some-
thing always comes
before. Maybe as meta-
phor. Planting the foot
down. Implies a previous

determination or re-
action to something already
passed by. Infers
the soil made ready,
the hole already dug. &
even when no planting
done, thinking about it
is a kind of prelude.

The Toledo *ficcione*

Willard J. Daniels re-
    putedly named
Toledo after the
    city in Spain
famous for its steel
because it "is easy to
    pronounce, is
pleasant in sound,
& there is no other city
    of that name on the
American continent." The
    reality is he was
    a dreamer, foresaw
the design of cities
in the future, blue-
printed a glass industry
for Ohio, assumed the
    easy association be-
tween the common name
    would conjoin their
outputs. Steel + glass
inevitably = skyscrapers.

Götterdämmerung

I wake up late.

Dylan Thomas is in the bed beside me.

He smells of liquor.

I am about to throw him out when he starts speaking.

His words don't get to me, but, oh, that Welsh accent.

I remember I liked him, long years ago.

Must have been when I was a windy boy & a bit.

I've moved on since, following neither that path

nor the road less traveled by.

Other avenues, other trees.

Sometimes, though, when the winds die down

& dreams are thin on the ground

you can hear the old voices.

Even though they no longer speak to you

you pause & listen to them.

intertwine

She chose the
double bass
as

the
invisible part
of herself. Now,

her intimate, low
register, haunting
songs

that
emphasize the
androgyny of emotion

are recognized as
a personal
trademark.

To Jukka, on holiday in Heinola

There was an owl in the garden last night, showing up as a moving patch of gray in the dark hollows between the palmtrees. It paused on a low branch about two meters above the ground & ten meters from where I sat having a cigarette. Turned its back on me when I turned a flashlight on it.

I haven't got around to planting bananas yet; but the pineapples are coming along in a piece of what was overgrown undergrowth that I cleared especially for them. Several varieties. No fruit yet, not even a central stalk; but the leaves are glossy green & increasing in size. All this from the small piece of core that remained when the crown was twisted off. Plugged into the soil. Watered well.

How's it going in Heinola, fixing the cabin, digging the well? Hope you don't get blisters on your palmpilot hands. Holiday cabins in New Zealand are generally built near the beach. You'll love what the local name for them is. Pronounced "batch" but spelt "bach."

I've sent Eileen the bio notes & a short publicity piece called *A True History of the Oracular Sonnets*. So everything's in place.

Am leaving for Auckland in a couple of days, off to be a public poet for the first time in thirty years. You gone north, me going south. Even closer to our respective Poles. But what's another thousand or so kilometers between friends? Distance is a relative thing.

Will write again soon.

Catnipped

He often
talked to the
cat, thought
nothing of it

until one after-
noon when, after
some cursory
chitchat about

the weather, she
asked him for
either a course
of hormone re-

placement therapy
or a karaoke machine
or, preferably, both
so that she could

properly celebrate
some previously
undocumented
feline festival.

a mixture of states

Schrödinger's dog perceived
objects in their right forms

but could not comprehend any
extortion attempt if multi-

disciplinary construction projects
were used in the commission of

the crime & may or may not have
come from stolen customer data.

banned mots

I'm allowed to say in
my reports that you
might have bubonic
plague, said the Secretary
of Health & Human
Services, *but I'm not*
allowed to say what
other pandemics
you're vulnerable to.

The Assistant Secretary
for Health concurred.
Diversity is not permitted.
Why do you think we
talk about the universe?
& entitlement to know-
ledge is not a right, it's
a privilege of rank, added
the Surgeon-General.

A Greek Chorus, in
lockstep, all wearing
Anonymous masks
& T-shirts with the
message ~~transgender~~
on them, entered the
office of the Federal
Budget Director. *I am*
an unborn child not

a fetus, they sang. *Life*
left me behind. So did
we, admitted the CDC
Director. *You were lost*
in translation. We mis-

read "intelligent design"
as "evidence-based" &
decided there was no
place available for you.

Outside the Verdant
Meadows Funeral Home
in Atlanta is a sign that
says *Go Out in Style at a*
budget price. &, slightly
smaller: *In Coffins, Caskets*
& Urns that have fallen
out of favor because their
design is science-based.

Art Informel

Art Informel

(Tachisme) is now a method used by
camouflage textile designers to
describe the patchy style
of the latest military garb for
killing people without being seen first.

Am I prepared to face the
tachiste revolution
I know is coming?

Am I weapon'd enough?

Are my sinews
sufficiently strong to use
as a rope ladder to
climb up to Paradise &
find there a bible, a folded
flag, an autographed photo
of the President & the
obligatory letter that
accompanies it?

Will I be able to read it
without weeping? Will
I recognize myself?

What happened to the
seven virgins I was
promised? Did the President
get there before me? Is
that where the flowers
at my funeral come from?

Am I still on the electoral rolls in Florida?

A note for Alex Gildzen

The studio system still
in operation in the
'fifties. A flagship blonde
contracted to each. Mamie
van Doren one studio's
answer to Jayne Mansfield
who, in turn, was that
studio's answer to
Marilyn Monroe; though
who was who's you'd
know better than I. & of
the three, the one
who at some point
accompanied my teenage
boylust was Jayne Mansfield,
strutting her stuff
in *The Girl Can't Help It*. Not
her that turned me on, though;
was Little Richard
singing the title song
that flicked my switch.

I was this frightened fifteen years ago. Imagine how I'm feeling now.

I have conscious memories of every U.S. President since Harry Truman.

I remember Eisenhower warning about the growth of the U.S. military-industrial complex.

I have lived through the Cold War, the Korean War, the war in Vietnam, Desert Storm.

I have heard U.S. generals advocate nuclear strikes on North Korea & North Vietnam. Reason prevailed.

I have seen the U.S. topple regimes through covert operations, prop up regimes, assist regimes because it suited them, stand by & do nothing when they should have been doing something.

The U.S. supported the Mujahaddin who later became the Taliban, supported Iraq against Iran, because it suited them at the time.

The U.S. did not support the nationalist policies of Tito, Castro or Ho Chi Minh because they perceived them as communist. They destroyed Allende.

Johnson lied about the Gulf of Tonkin. Forty years later Bush lied about the weapons of mass destruction. Nixon just lied.

Jimmy Carter seems to me to have been the only ethical President the U.S. has had in the last 40 years. Which is probably why he only lasted four years in the job.

I find less horror in 9/11 than I do in the nuclear bombings of Hiroshima & Nagasaki, than I do in the genocide in Cambodia, in Rwanda, in the former Yugoslavia.

I can find no justification for any armed incursion by the U.S. since the second world war.

I cannot be the only one who views what Israel is doing to the Palestinians as criminal, who sees that the blind eye that the U.S. turns continues to fuel those activities.

So much has gone on over the years that has disturbed me; & yet I have never been so frightened by the actions taken by the U.S. as I have been by those taken under the current President's administration.

I am terrified of what will happen if Bush is re-elected.

A Small Compendium

High summer
is such an
elegant phrase

but he kept
a small
compendium
of winter

on hand
for days

like this.

on the edge

The rumors that the Gillette Corporation were looking to sue the estate of the late William of Occam, alleging that their trademark had been impinged upon, are true. Also true is the accompanying news report that their legal team had become so bogged down in precedents of increasing complexity that they saw no way forward until a junior member suggested that the best method for preparing their case was to select the simplest argument & proceed from there.

Songs to Come for the Salamander

Axolotls can breed whilst still remaining tadpoles.

Hellbenders, mudpuppies, waterdogs, sirens.

There are nine
families of salamander,
some 300 species.

Andrias japonicus
is five feet long.

Lungless salamanders. Mole salamanders.

Salamandra salamandra
is black with bright yellow,
orange, or red markings.

Newts.

Neoteny is the retention of some juvenile characteristics
in an animal that seems otherwise mature.

Axolotls will only metamorphose into
adult salamanders when their ponds dry up.

The salamander is impervious to fire.

Tips from the pioneers

In their pristine state
even the most benign-
looking lithium-ion-
battery is based on a
predatory concept. Its
diet is composed of
elements such as salt-
bush, grass, plants; its

mires sequester large a-
mounts of atmospheric
carbon dioxide; it has
always been in a con-
stant state of flux. Tie
dying a t-shirt can be a
scary idea. Carnivory
increases the fuel load.

A Glass of Champagne

Tell the truth. The com-
petition of long ago still

haunts. Her hair shimmers.
Problems of the past should

be a thing of the past. Are
you on board with that?

Provided you lie about it she
shot back. A violin trembles,

the telephone rings. They
walk out to buy noodles.

The transition of Cold-Dryness

I really love getting my
eyebrows done by my
psychiatrist. I have not

eaten all day; have gently
filled my colon with warm
filtered water; have spent

the afternoon filling in
crossword puzzles. Years
pass quickly & my eye-

brows keep growing. Time
to visit my shrink & fill
the room with foul odors.

the urban landscape

La discontinuité sémantique
encloses a world of war-
time horror & diminishing

salt marshes. There is al-
ways a consensual orgy
of *schadenfreude.* That

picture is filed under "Home
& Garden & Crafts." & nobody
has yet conceptualized dystopia.

Evangelical associations

Military forces of
all nations switched
to a 6-hour day last

week, saying they
wanted to spend
more time with

their families. It
appears to be
a software glitch.

The PATRIOT ACT offers

Designer glasses, sunglasses, contact lenses, & eye care.
A 50,000-mile sign-up bonus, & you can transfer the miles to airline partners.
Donuts & coffee free to the value of $150 to the first person in the line.
A whorehouse without a second floor, which makes erection easy.

Women's work suits designed for a Central American city lifestyle.
Open-ended questions for which there are many wrong answers.
Utopian/dystopian texts about an all-female society.
Levels of experience that enhance the spike output of neocortical neurons.
Dacoity as a rural crime wth a strong element of social & economic protest.

Hedonism without the epistemic arguments that add little to the pleasure.
An additional $2 million in bonuses for starts in each of the next two seasons.
Valedictories to long-forgotten deities evoked to provide a patina of respectability.
Exploitation of one's position for financial benefit &/or sexual favors.

Lighter-than-air devices that can withstand living in a vacuum.
Orgone Energy Accumulators at rock-bottom prices.
Vanity boxes that serve double duty as gun safes.
Erudite arguments, supported with obscure biblical references.
Dedicated channels as an optimal network support for effective transfer of massive data.

Attitudes toward gender dysphoria that are rooted in the Dark Ages.

DEFCON 2 military wear & accessories in red, white, & blue,
stars & stripes optional.
Authoritative translations into Aramaic with example sentences
& audio pronunciations.
Yarrow stalks to assist in making decisions which you don't
want to be responsible for.

Little Bo Peep Blouses to inject some whimsy into the rendition
of "enemy combatants."
Independent medical services, delivering definitive information
to enable optimal decisions.
Kodak moments to share with your loved ones — if you ever get
to see them again.
Exciting opportunities for those with detention center
experience.

Twelve centuries of Vatican highlights provided in a
comprehensive & exclusive kit.
Hints of oak fermentation. Aroma of lemon oil & zest, candle
wax & smoke. Cut hay.
Imprecise arguments so that fuzzy logic will prevail.
Saturday nights that are alright for fighting & to get a little
action in.

damp trumpets

Today the
postman brought
me a military
parade down
Pennsylvania
Avenue. I was
so disappointed.
Where are the
submarines? I
shouted out. *You*
promised you'd
drain the swamp
so I'd be able
to see the submarines
that were lying
on the bottom.

turning to drones

Leaving behind your familiar house

Winter on the mainland can
be an enormously stressful
time. Antelopes stand on their
hind legs to reach the acacia
leaves, hoping to break the Yin
or Yang down into its essential
five elements. Freud hid his work
from Jung at first, considered it

a difficult & painful topic, some-
thing he wasn't comfortable
talking about to his mother. In-
stead offered up a compilation
of therapy tips & techniques
gleaned from 17 years training.

monkey canapes

In order to stop kids
obsessing over the future,
Government funding is

now available to separate
them into groups &
place them on a range of

intimate couches in front
of refrigerators which all
have smart screens & apps.

Deconstructing Dickens

It was the best of
times—all the big-
name philosophers
were in the room.

It was the worst
of times—he didn't
understand a word
they were saying.

Survivisection

A coal stove burns
in the corner. I don't
want a coal stove. In
a survival situation,
versatility is essential.

Knife, ax & machete –
these items are extremely
necessary. Other minimal
lists have taken the count-
ing challenge to the limit.

I now own 15 things. *Je
veux un hamburger.* "Yes.
Much as I expected." The
other eats, hates himself
for eating, & then purges

it out. Houses are the best
places to hide out in. I exit
out of the tail with CTRL+C
& continue. Assume that
everything is case specific.

My biggest fear is that I'll
fall back down the hole.
Ramen noodles aren't the
most nutritional food but
they are cheap. & easy to

prepare. I no longer have
a coal stove or pots & pans
or water, but I watched
a video & now know how
to cook ramen in a cactus.

since violence is learned

The library platform is independent in all sections, apart from the young adult ministry niche. That's involved in environmental management matters — such as: can a fully veiled woman purchase a vehicle? — in addition to training multilingual staff to assist you with debugging

problems, & providing tour & ticket assistance. Soldiers encourage the youth to attend. The more aged & less mobile are taken away to be disposed of thoughtfully. Tolerance is no longer available, is replaced by trauma.

teflon eyes

Preschoolers get apple juice
at snack time. I just wanted
to exchange my eyes for the
teflon pair he kept in the desk
drawer. Plenty of these tools
have become available even
on the clear web; but he was
selfish with his, refused to give

them to me. We both got angry,
came to blows, took out our
knives. The potential fallout
could extend far beyond West
Virginia. Getting him on camera
would have been a scene saver.

Sorry, but I couldn't find a bottle

Try not to read too much into it. Certainly elephants are rare in these parts, & elephants giving birth even more so. But remember that here you're on the main road from nowhere to nowhere; & at the somewheres in between anything is a possibility.

After all there are still supposed sightings of the Tasmanian tiger & the local version of the yeti / sasquatch. Yowies they call them here. Just say to the Tourist Bureau on your way out of town that you saw a pachyderm. Anywhere else they might be astute enough to ask if it was Indian or African & get suspicious when you can't tell them where the tusks were relative to the ears.

Here they'll just record it as an unconfirmed sighting & include it in their next brochure as another reason to visit North Queensland. &, hopefully, someday someone out there in the Great Beyond will see the tourist brochure, recognize the hand behind the inherent absurdity of the claim, & say "So that's where Mark Young is living now."

Stuck inside of Mobile

I want too much, &
often take the same.

Economists tell me
this is wrong, a part

of it anyway, for
wants are unlimited

but resources scarce.
& so my prolifigacy

will cause prices to rise,
babies to starve, atolls

in the South Pacific to
submerge as temper-

atures increase in anger
at my actions. I turn away,

want not to know what
my wants might lead to.

Constant Craving

The day is spinning wildly
on its turntable, & even out
of it the vibrations can still
be clearly felt. I'm trapped in
what might as well be Mach-
iavellian Merchandise, a tent
in sideshow alley, where there's
nothing you want or need
or can afford but still feel
compelled to spend up big before
you go. Either by the purchase of
a cutprice epiphany that is not
yet spoken for—which in itself
is indicative of its value—or doing
a dodgy deal in wagyu beef
futures. Neither of which...

But I am brought down to
earth & saved from calamity
by a track squeezing through
from the dodgems next door,
k.d. lang singing *so in love,* the
Cole Porter song, that acts as
axis to steady everything around.

The Owls

There's always an audience
out there. It's just that some-
times you've got to go out
on a limb to pull them in.

Don't be subtle about it. Start
by covering the exterior walls
of your house with sheets of
corrugated iron painted in

primary colors. Wait until round
about midnight, then walk out
into the garden & begin reciting
your poems. This will infuriate

the owls. Poetry confuses them.
They're sure to retaliate, lay shit
on your renovations, stare at you
with those big wide eyes they

have & say: *You should have used
wood or adobe.* Or: *A delicate shade
of lime would have been much more
relaxing.* But keep at the poems

until the owls have finished
hooting at you, then point out
how the colors now make it easier
for them to separate the mice

from the surrounding shrubbery.
They will pause, then nod. It'll
be faint praise, but at least you
won't be damned by it, & with

a reliable food supply available
the owls will stick around. People
will come to see them. Some may
even stay & listen to your poetry.

wagasa

Idiosyncrasies float by below
me. The bridge ignores them,
instead turns & offers me

an *ukiyo-e* woodblock print
of the Sanjo Bridge that spans
the Kamo River. I hold it up

to the light. "Quite the self-
portrait," I say, "even though
it is of another time & place."

turpentine

IM'ing Yetunde

Yetunde is ranked No. 315 on TripAdvisor among its listed 788 virtual hostesses.

She was taught at an early age about the benefits of technology but leant later that it can dismember relationships.

Yetunde sells provisions & drinks to earn a living.

Her quest is to make Sendagaya the fashionable address within Shibuya-ku.

Yetunde has 213 books on Goodreads.

She thinks about getting a hamster &/or a tropical fish.

Yetunde says you can tell the love hotels — the *rabu hoteru* — by their bright-lit neon signs with funny names.

She spends much of her leisure time examining photos of New York graffiti, searches within them hoping to identify the beginnings of the paradigm shift that changed the city.

Yetunde wonders what life would be like if she were red & her ambitions were not so transparent.

She focuses upon a small portion of her emotions, then holds it up against a geographical background. What analogy comes up—what pictures does she see?

Pssst. / Wanna buy / a dirty bomb?

Well at least the
North Koreans
didn't blow up cities,
contaminate the marine
ecosystem of the
South Pacific, displace
people, force volunteers
to stand in the path
of the contaminant
winds……

But then, but
then. The question
must be asked. With
that frightening
plethora of marching
bands & a
chorus line that has
more people in it
than half the
nations on this
planet, why do they
feel the need to
have a nuclear
deterrent as well?

11.04 a.m.

The helicopters come
rotoring in. Which means:
not rescue operations but
war games. & since it
seems that most of the

Australian Armed Forces
are either overseas in
Syria or Afghanistan at
Trump's behest, or in-
volved in trials accused of

cat-killing, bastardization,
or drug abuse, I suppose
we should be pleased
that soon the jets of the
Singaporean Air Force

will come screaming down
the valley upsetting
the mosquitoes & injecting
much needed millions
into the local economy.

The Cooling Pond

When power plants throw
away the same amount of
waste heat as the energy
they generate, a search for a

fixed point is pure instru-
mental indulgence. So many
targets; no way to tell
when the process will end

if one begins considering
spiritual questions seriously.
On the cooling pond black
swans glide by. A harpist

plays Pachelbel's *Canon
in D Minor*. A man & a
woman share a telephone
line. They despise each other.

In a Bangkok bar

A flock of geese in
silent protest. The
balcony at dawn.

His question angered
her. Something about
an old brass fitting.

She was no good at
driving. The para-
medics arrived first.

The overlap

The dichotomy that
is Cyndi Lauper in
garish technicolor
in a documentary
on a pre-MTV music
show opining girls
just want to have fun

&, two doors up on a
World Movies channel,
Toshiro Mifune in the
melodramatic black &
white of *Throne of Blood*—
Kurosawa's take on the
Bard's "Scottish play"—

is somewhat shattered
when you notice the in-
ear headphones on the
manipulative Lady Macbeth
& the way her lips move
in time with the words of
the Cyndi Lauper song.

Concerning

Steam, & the spattering
of water, form kanji
characters on the sliding

shower door. The first
grouping says *veri-
similitude*; the second

says *finality*. The third—
even though you live
in the tropics—says

*there'll be a snow plough
doing the rounds very
early, tomorrow morning.*

Grace note

What do we write about
at the beginning, at the end?

Two periods of fifteen years.
Twenty-five years of silence

in between. Began by writing
about lizards. Have come

back to them again. Outlived
the earlier ones. The later ones

will probably outlive me. What
is the angle of a turning circle?

is suggestive of

I go to the Issuu site
of the issue of a
journal I am in

& am invited to
let lots of hot
russian ladies

grow my business
on line, & am also
let know that beaut-

iful thai ladies are
available to marry me
if I convert to a pdf.

On TCM

I watch the
forties
Cole Porter
bio-pic in
which a
gay man

pretending
he isn't plays
a gay man
pretending
he isn't. Only
the music

is forth-
coming, &
I have k.d.
lang to
thank for
that.

from Simple to Sublime

As sites rise to the surface, the
only option is to avoid foods
that may cause the release of
confidential documents. Our
website has not worked as well
as it could, needed a couple
of pie charts in there, to really
demonstrate the poor financial

health of News Corp even after
fifty thousand homeless people
were moved into a chic studio
apartment in an NYC townhouse &
given sheets of newspaper to sleep
beneath during the World Cup.

how / much can / a grizzly bear

Oil prices slipped on
Friday, just in time for
the girls' drama & gymnastics
classes. Now two of the
three ratings agencies
agree: the summer cruise
season coincides with
hurricane season. We
celebrate the music of
The Grateful Dead with
armed conflicts & suicide
attacks, advertise it on
Guns America creating
both novel social inter-
actions between bats
& humans & Billboard-
charting albums. Support
for the Perseid meteor
shower with the eBay
seller community is
building to a peak. Eco-
systems need improvised
explosions & aerial
bombardments. Ian is
a male model. Ian is a
bicycle rider. August
is an endurance race
for the trail warrior.

The early Clint Eastwood

What the hell am I doing
here? Should have signed
up for another television
season. But no, I had to go
& listen to *Sketches of Spain*
& thought Iberia might be
an exciting place to make

a movie in. Then again it
could have been the way
that Sergio & that composer
with the fag-sounding name
wined & dined me before I
signed the deal. I mean,
imagine it. There I am in

this fancy Italian restaurant,
eating all these dishes
named after painters I'd
never ever heard of,
washing them down with
a not-so-delicate green
of a *nouvelle vague* mintage

& being pitched the concept
of a western whose script
was ripped from some
Japanese samurai movie.
Not only that — the hero
has no name & very little
to say, smokes cigarillos,

wears a hat that looks like
it was stolen from a Quaker
& has this thing around

his shoulders that they call
a *serape* but seems more like
a throw-down hall rug to me.
No mention of the sand, the

standing around like melting
mannequins in the heat, the
fact that nobody but me speaks
English. I can't wait for the
shooting to be over. No way
I'm coming back. This was
never a good career move.

the dowager's asswipe

The alcohol-metabolizing penis weapons —humpback or hump raven — astonishes nova. We don't have chickenpox in my minibus. At last we were ushered to our select table.

(content was: '{{delete}}Amateur was founded by the Rosi Cross foundation in 1892 and has since evolved into a popular discourse, whereby morse code is transmitted...')

This much dyspnea. Him, it, they, she. Amalgam or amalgam fillings, dermatosis in voluminous autism. Legman, bukowski, ganja, mammoth, riverrat. ...

(content was: '{{delete}}Early Days & Latter Days is a collection of the greatest hits of Led Zeppelin.'

Nine year old girl missing in SD due to ineptitude of childrens home, likely an icecube. Now Una was lucky, she'd get a clean, quick death. She would need lots of cats.

(content was: 'Mikeee, is a cockney wankerMuswell hill is a shithole where he lives. He fucking sucks!!!{{delete}}')

When you purchase an awesome DK Star Wars book, you can also get your very own paper-engineered, posable, 3-D droid!

(content was: '{{delete}}sauna from sauna')

Nude Studio Pic - Estira Doble. Prostitute Footjob & a dozen of her poems. Inventor-scientist movie-buffs semi-realistic somersaulting anesthetist. A tired "toothless" media hack.

(content was: '{{delete}}I think I accidentally re-created this page.'))

from 1750 words

from 1750 words
#1

Clear as it may seem to be
men do not shape destiny.

Move in then, reset the paradoxes.
They seem to have stopped working.

In the case of the closure of an entity
there are no products matching the selection.

Is, since it is either a sense of guilt
or. Simply to engage in a distinctive

& familiar

way in which
expressed behavior has faded &

information leaked away in order
to grow low-impact herbs.

Su Shi, a famous Song Dynasty poet, said, " It is a return to the
time before time, & historical timelines with inaccurate calendars
can have significant impact without adding unreasonably to
your costs."

#6

It seems so simple
this sense of
shaking off desire.

So many years
with a
nimbus at salient.

Now to begin
dismantling
the self, using

the negative. Not so
easy changing
the status quo.

#7

An awesome app! & at
such a low price! Can be
operated from the comfort
of your own cardboard

container. It reminds me
of some form of soft em-
balmer. Inevitably fatal, but
you take some time to die.

 # 14 (actions & comments)

: needles will turn :
: the leaf :
: embellished by the tropics :

she looked more of a child than

: a drug to treat many people :
: well suited for cold weather :
: you can find better detail in shadows :

After, (WCW) befriends a co-worker
who also DJs on the side.

Most paint symbols on
Were intercepted by
Will actually kind of go towards

the loose swing & the obsessive grinding

Nature maintained a close
relationship with the enemy.

#17

The
 Canopic?

: transactions or

their site?

The Egyptians
could.
                                        Cloud.
The jar
a way through.

Curtails.
: with a long object :

: with other
objects :

has

: turpentine.

Curtains.

#18 (Prostrate)

The newspaper group has
been exposed by showing
internal operating accounts:

diving profits for its tabloids /
swingeing job cuts /
subcontract squandering.

Customers laughing at
them will only cause
further damage. So, too,

a predominant tendency —
Australians returning
from foreign war zones.

#25

and all you

Especially.
the building
he
Shop today for the best
are.
.
Find.
produce is a
Surprise arrival of frustrates applicants
.
on their
anything they can.
they

There are also
we are showing is the vigilance
a
' '
, but on Owsla they
.
atmosphere and ambience
chills
Scutenaire who thought of the title, may no doubt have
remembered that in the dictionary the entry 'Violin' explains
what the violin is made of, in particular its 'âme' ('soul' in
French, refers to the sound post for a violin) and the word 'âme'
may have reminded him of a book he read long ago: 'A little of
the outlaws' souls' and made him decide that the book-title
fitted the picture."
— René Magritte's letter to H. Torczyner

spasmodic submissive   infantile

#28

Vibrations play a critical role.

Nothing goes to discussion
except for the occasional
mistakes by the speaker.

Water hammer taken dripping
can generate pressure
transients. It would

unfortunately create a dead leg.

Everything is connected.

#29

Big dams without navigation locks are
very sparse on our 12 acre property in
the foothills of Western North Carolina.

Levi-Strauss' answer is practical: the idea that
members of a particular religious group are under
no obligation to obey the laws of ethics or morality

lies in a longitudinal direction & is composed of
an angular frame that lends the tender nude an
explosive force, a general boorishness. Not only

does it resist smog but, like the *bricoleur,* one
can use it as an opposition while accepting it as
a philosophical truth in many civil rights issues.

#31 (*misugaru* in korean)

On tasting the hands of human

due to the
may be obtained by .
Acquires Terracotta...
she.

as

This includes understanding

It's really just
inscription
context

little

when
them , , , which he claims

#32 (has been relentless.)

bold

The acidity, the sweetness,
continue to be usually
set up in the early morning

have been

tough infantry from the frontier with Islam

After the *Rolling Stone* article was written:

Under no circumstances shall the End-user
be entitled to transfer to any other party
the typefaces &/or fonts.

All the invitations had been sent out,
the answers received.

Tags: manga, conga line, QAnon, anarchy.

the conqueror

The Toast

A Recipe

Start with a word. Any word.
Or a phrase, even if it's in
Greek or Latin & so obscure
that you have to go back & look up
the meaning of it after only a couple
of days. Start with anything; but
if it seems to be leading to a
dead end, then fence it off with
* * * * * * *
& move on. With another word
or phrase. A sentence even. It
doesn't need to relate to what's
gone on before, doesn't even
need to make sense. Some
thing may fall out of it, several
things perhaps. Or reprise the
first phrase, invert it as if it were
a Bach canon. Even if you still
can't remember what it means
you might recall what you meant
by it. It gives you pause either
way, a breathing space in your
line of thought; & from here on in
you can improvise, embellish, go
off on a tangent, imagine you are
Jean Genet writing the script for a
travelogue. Add anecdotes. Quote
or misquote from others. Leave
road signs for later travelers
but cover them with graffiti until
the original meaning is obscured.

Let stand for thirty years.

One for the Border Force

So maybe you take the chance
& walk out across the sand &
into the sea. Maybe
they won't notice you there
among the dervish gulls, think
you're a rock or a resting
seal. & even if they do they
probably won't care. Their
job is to stop people
from coming ashore, not to
stop the malcontents from
leaving. Just don't turn around
& try coming back.

retrograde condensate

As a flockmeister / most
of her caprices involved
the works of Patrick White.

Hands neatly tucked away out of sight.

It is very important at the
beginning to send out a DVD
of a Nuclear Blast — deliberate
capitalization — *to demonstrate*
the true character of retro-
grade dogmas. (Amos, 5:24)

MICE — meetings, incentives, conventions &
exhibitions — become a hazard for drivers.

Try adding more information.
Unfortunately, too many com-
puters are unsure what that is.

Is said the strength of Biscuit,
of Crunt & Biscuit, lies in his
opening his mouth real wide.

Daisy irae

A small shiny-black beetle
crawls across the inside
of the car window. The field
is being prepared for rice. We
watch a riverboat move in waltz
time along the highway. A stop-
light sings silently to itself.

Fill / loosely & / do not compact

With experience, this copper-alloy piece can be used to create a product that includes all the processes involved in harvesting, production, transportation, & construction. It eliminates all extremes of elaboration, but forces you to leave behind your familiar house, street, & neighbors; & prompts a defection from fixed meaning through the use of non-sequiturs — start off with Magritte & move on to the navigational abilities of the prostate, from Derrida on to the venture capital industry.

she calmed down after she'd finished talking

Anger had got the better of that
"o" often found at the ending
of Australian nicknames. Else-
where, over the fence, two young
girls sing each example of that We
will, we will rock you line from
the Queen song. They are dread-
fully out of tune, as if part of

a conspiracy whose aim is to
utilize misshapen counterpoint
as a way of moving minds away
from — not so much the current
pandemic but the paucity of the
responses to it. Negative energies
accumulate in the corners. Even
feng shui can't drive them away.

geographies: New York City

The new pro-breast milk
policy stigmatizes colored
glass & provides less leg
room for creatives to put
their ideas out on the table.

geographies: Teluk Ambun

A green man on a bi-
cycle, with a huge
body & tiny bungalow,

followed the peloton
on the route along
Trikora Beach. She

was peaceful & air-
conditioned. Nobody
had much money at

the time. Logical
errors are the hardest
kind of errors to find.

geographies: **Istanbul**

Women's made to
measure flare pants,
with an aroma

of light oak
& dark fruit,
were built by

Numarine in Gebze
& intended to convert
the U.S. Nuclear Naval

Fleet away from endangered
pecan turtles & across
to red velvet cupcakes.

geographies: Palau

Scaffolding creates remote-
ness, mixes crossbows with

sand to improve moisture
retention, even after the

safety has been re-engaged.
An electrolyte imbalance

means the dome light keeps
flashing; visible seaweed in-

dicates low water level. Soak
the kelp in a jacuzzi to keep

it androgynous & the vision-
ary crabjuice business viable.

geographies: Ciudad Bolivar

Now that the instruments
of the national orchestra
have been turned into
mulch for the cacoa
plantations, it's easy to
see why US president
Donald Trump's decision
to send a task force of
egregious windmills into
Venezuala to resolve the
country's political crisis
was anathema to the
local musical community.

geographies: **Antalya**

One of the hubs in this so-
called cradle of civilization is a

treasure house of circum-
cized single USB ports. It also

includes a kitchen that uses an
obscure cosmic emanation known

as "fast radio bursts" to facilitate the
production of their artisanal craft

beers which are now available
in cans & bottles or on tap.

the character killed off early

I have a charcoal grill made
of hand painted high-quality
resin with several different
mounting options. It's really
important to let others know

what one possesses — I've
been hiding who I am for so
long. Feedback is necessary,
especially now that I'm part-
icipating in so many Zoom

meetings courtesy of my new
gooseneck camera. Motors
must be single phase, familiar
with the key knowledge dot
points, & printed on thick 100

pound quality paper. Weak
AI, neither measured nor bil-
led, could cause disruptions
in the electric grid. Please
enter your model number.

A line from Henry Ford

Focus attention on the
illegal gun. Know how to
ride a bike. War is a risky
get-rich-quick scheme

if you're afraid of the stock
market. The French terror
maniacs met often with
poetry, had an infinite

capacity for some modern
Mexican poets, particularly
a wild-eyed Latina whose
exposé of the links between

Kentucky coal mines & organ-
ized crime explains why rich
people have such chicken-
shit long term memory.

A line from René Magritte

It's a bleak view of hu-
manity. Facing eco-
logical collapse, Freddo,
plus a whole host of

Cadbury characters, went
beyond science to shine
a spotlight on transgender
issues, using their jittery

art-punk guitar buzz to
offer a frayed life-line to
the most vulnerable people.
The snowoman wonders

what the world offers them
outside of that. An ability
to handle subzero temper-
atures? They have that already.

landscape with proscenium arch

Center stage is an orange caricature, a man muttering about "vicious dogs" & "ominous weapons." Something of a bully who, unfortunately, has a bully pulpit to play with, that incorporates a prompt or two from which he reads — badly & with an obvious lack of understanding of their meaning — the words of those others who he thinks, for the time being at least, are on his side. His head is cocked, like a bird listening for worms, only without any signs of innate intelligence.

There is noise offstage. Suddenly secret service agents come rushing in to the room, form a phalanx around him, & escort him to the confines of the in-house bunker. For some time there is silence, then the bird returns, tweeting incessantly.

The Toast

Shortly, & with
little warning, the
pools of hypocrisy
ice over & become
malevolent. We are
back in St. Petersburg,
never having been
here before, but I
recognize the
ghosts. "Such pretty
lizards," she said, then
raised her glass in
the general direction
of the sky. *"Za vashe
zdorovye."* It was
a formal toast. No
story followed.

The Sasquatch Walks Among Us

From the Pound *Cantos*: CENTO I

I slept in Circe's ingle. Unburied, unwept,
unwrapped in sepulchre. These many
crowded about me, with shouting. & in

the water, the almond-white swimmers.
Dawn, to our waking, drifts in the green
cool light. The sunlight glitters, glitters

atop forked branch-tips, flaming as if
with lotus, the bride awaiting the god's
touch. & beneath the jazz a cortex, a

stiffness or stillness. The angle almost
imperceptible, the calm field, the
grass quiet. The house a shade too solid,

a dryness calling for death, knocking at
empty rooms, seeking for buried beauty.

The handsomest man in Washington society was also a serial adulterer

Remarkably, researchers believe the cliques are formed for social reasons rather than for supplies of coal, are largely controlled by the government, have not been enough to meet the focus on reducing overheads, operating costs & non-essential expenditures. A perfect tragedy should, as we have seen, be arranged not on the simple but on the complex plan. To arm increasing miles, non-spongers, & associates of the solar powder & excite pity & fear, this being the distinctive mark of tragic imitation. Plants overhead were the downfall of the utter villain whose misfortune is brought about not by vice or depravity but who exhibits several ties of kinship or friendship with inhuman (sub)cultures said to be better at maintaining alliances & infrastructure, including almost all those tool-using dolphins who prefer others like themselves, strongly suggesting that sponge grids included excessive demands placed from certain regions, due in part to the arm preferentially associating with others who share its subculture & who can then sieve more mega-projects until economic outlooks improve the samples & deliver critical role fine powder to instruments inside the rover for a thorough analysis. Like humans who generate more electricity, tool-use relying on more coal is a cultural behaviour, further centralizing the embarrassing reminder of a nation's energy infrastructure. It was not art, but happy chance, that led the poets in search of subjects to impress the tragic quality upon their plots. It was proposed only a day after another change of fortune & a major power failure that the event, therefore, will be neither pitiful nor a terrible consequence of similarity but a socially learned trait, a scenario that resonates with human culture. They said. "Spongers were more cliquish, had more sponger associates & stronger bonds with generators as well as yawning power shortages & an absence of governmental action." Some 300 million people have no access to relative cost curves at all, & 300 million more have only sporadic recourse to those houses whose history contains perfect incidents according to the moving rules of art. Nothing can be more alien to the spirit of coalition government.

Asylum seekers question offshore threat

Know this, America. Our problems can be solved. Our challenges can be met. The path we offer may be harder, but it leads to a better place. His earlier lecture was a compelling plea in favour of legalizing gay marriage; on Wednesday he addressed the issues of truth, trust & the general degradation of our politics. After that, they staged an orgy in a public place. Of course, people are allowed to do whatever they want to do, as long as it's legal, but this kind of conduct in a public place should not go unnoticed by the manufacturing, energy, education, & national security authorities. I'm asking you to upload all the time. Makers of consumer electronics are refreshing their products for the holiday shopping season, a real, achievable plan that will lead to new jobs, more opportunity, & rebuild this economy on a stronger foundation. I'm asking you to choose that future. While he declined to say what the cause was or in which room the fire had begun, he said rumors there had been a drug lab present in the building were untrue.

Stayin' alive

Break off doing
what I'm doing

go outside
for a cigarette —
note to self: I
should have a
macro for that —

& listen to
L. listening to
the Bee Gees in
the room above

sound system
positioned just so

downward sound

so that you are
standing in a spot
where everything
is spotlessly clear

— albeit falsetto —

& disregarding
the high voices
the disco sound of it
John T. strutting
down the street
in that wide-lapeled
Italian suit

(no mirror ball

here / no need
for reflection)

realize that
it's not filters
that strain the
background noise
like a whale
sieving krill

but an ability
even as you
are moving

to recognize
that single still point
where the noise
divides &
the song
breaks through.

Quick! before the stream dries up completely

Accident
Identikit

Axolotl
Idolatry

Axiom
Idiom

Axle
Idle

Ax
Id

A
I

From the Pound *Cantos*: CENTO III

The hooves, moving in
heavy air, clink & slick
on the cobbles. Palace in

smoky light. Hard night, &
parting at morning. Not a ray,
not a slivver, not a spare disc

of sunlight. Thin husks I had
known as men, weaving an
endless sentence, propped

between chairs & table. &
then went down to the
ship, mad for a little slave

money, winds stretching out,
seas pulling to eastward.

WITH BASHŌ ON THE FRONT PORCH

furuike ya
kawazu tobikonu
mizu no oto
Bashō Mitsuo

Light rain, & the sounds that come with it. Drops leaking from leaf to leaf or sizzling on the high voltage lines that run behind the house. Chordal structure of two tones of cicada noise above the deeper sound that is rainwater trickling into a drain across the road. A single frog.

"Pumpkins," he said. " I'd have to include something like that since it's autumn, & seasonal ciphers are expected of a *haijin,* a *haiku* poet like myself. & even these simple events that now surround us have a continuity I am not allowed — unless, of course, I'm writing with someone else, trading verses back & forth like in that poem by Gregory Corso about poets hitchhiking on the highway. *Hokku, haikai, haiku* — they're all the same with their restrictions & constrictions. I've turned into an incidental poet, have become a travel writer who uses poems instead of photographs."

A pause as he lit the cigarette I'd given him. "Each time I put brush to paper I am confronted by that old head / heart conundrum. The head knows how to use one or two lines to sketch the surroundings, then puncture them with an observation that occurs at right angles to everything else around. It's the Zen thing, the *A-ha*

effect; & I am good at it & comfortable
with both form & style. But the heart
still dreams of poems that have no
formal structure, that are / full of music, that
burst forth with the energy of the downpour
that came through here an hour ago."

Then he laughed." Enough of this fanciful
talk. I'd better go & judge that *haiku*
competition that brought me over here
in he first place." & set off down the path,
moving quietly, without disturbing anything.

The frog croaks again
Staff in the traveler's hand
mizu no oto

The sound of water

The Sasquatch walks among us

Apart from the very white
guy who walks by wearing a
black T-shirt with a simple
"Muhammad Ali" printed on it,
half the world wears baseball
tees even if they come from the
half of the world that either
doesn't play the game or know
what it's about. That's why I
feel safe getting around in a
bannered shirt that lauds the
virtues of Nietzsche & his
Nihilist Muskrats. The op-
probium inherent in it rarely
registers. One half thinks that
NM is a term that comes from
curling. The other half congrat-
ulate themselves on knowing
things outside their area of ex-
pertise, that they recognize this
famous gridiron team that hails
from — is it? — the Appalachians.

pelican, dreaming

Shee-it! The
pelican's been
reading Yeats
again, getting
into that gyre
thing. Riding
thermals in the
sky, spiraling
wider & higher,
spread wings
not beating,
dreaming
it's a falcon.

Pelican Dreaming Revisited

Today the
postman brought
me a postcard
of Venice, sent
by one of the
pelicans that
usually lives
on the lagoon
at the bottom
of the street.
"Strange to be
fishing through
a culture that's
only a few
thousand years

old," she wrote. "But
easy to see how
the Europeans
managed to fuck
Australia over in
just a couple of
centuries after we'd
looked after it for
60,000 years. Look at
this place. Effluent
in the lagoon, dead
fish, houses
in decay or sinking
below the water-
line. Gone to the
doges, as the locals
say. Still, it's great
to be a cultural
nomad for a
while. Paris
last week, the
Greek Isles next. Now
& again I have to
pinch myself, just
to make sure I'm
not dreaming."

From the Pound *Cantos*: CENTO V

Sound drifts in the evening haze,
North wind nips on the bough;
& in small house by town's edge—

slung like an ox in smith's sling—
now was wine-trunk here stripped,
here made to stand, stilling the ill

beat music. A young man walks,
grave incessu, at church with
galleried porch, drinking the tone

of things. Brown-yellow wood,
& the no-color plaster, all flat on
the ground now, making mock of

the inky faithful. When you take
it, give me a slice. A poet's ending.

Books by Mark Young

Text Poetry

Blues for New Lovers, The Poets' Co-operative, Auckland, N.Z., 1968
The right foot of the giant, Bumper Books, Wellington, N.Z., 1999
The Oracular Sonnets (with Jukka-Pekka Kervinen), Meritage Press, California, U.S.A., 2004
Sun Moon's Mother, PI books, Washington, D.C., U.S.A., 2004
calligraphies, xPressed, Espoo, Finland, 2004
Poles Apart (with Jukka-Pekka Kervinen), xPressed, Espoo, Finland, 2004
The Cicerone, xPressed, Espoo, Finland, 2005
sur la plage, Capricornia Poets, Yeppoon, Australia, 2005
from Series Magritte, Moria Books, Chicago, U.S.A., 2006
Betabet, BlazeVox Books, Boston, U.S.A., 2006
episodes, xPressed, Espoo, Finland, 2006
Falsely Goethe, Otoliths, Rockhampton, Australia, 2007
Lunch Poems, Soapbox Press, Auckland, N.Z., 2008
Pelican Dreaming: Selected Poems 1959-2008, Meritage Press, California, U.S.A., 2008
more from Series Magritte, Moria Books, Chicago, U.S.A., 2009
terracotta worriers, ungovernable press, Malmo, Sweden, 2009
Genji Monogatari, Otoliths, Rockhampton, Australia, 2010
At Trotsky's Funeral, Kilmog Press, Dunedin, N.Z., 2010
some Geographies, Argotist Ebooks, Liverpool, U.K., 2010
Geographies, Dysphasia Press, Detroit, U.S.A., 2011
The Codicils, Otoliths, Rockhampton, Australia, 2013
Asemic Colon, The Red Ceilings Press, Derbyshire, U.K., 2013
the eclectic world, gradient books, Finland, 2014
HOTUS POTUS, Meritage Press, California, U.S.A., 2015
A small compendium of bats, Swirl mag & editions, Malmo, Sweden, 2015
Bandicoot Habitat, gradient books, Finland, 2015
lithic typology, gradient books, Finland, 2016

The Holy Sonnets unDonne, The Red Ceilings Press, Derbyshire, U.K., 2016
Mineral Terpsichore, gradient books, Finland, 2016
The Chorus of the Sphinxes, Moria Books, Chicago, U.S.A., 2016
For the Witches in Romania, Beard of Bees, Oak Park and Chicago, U.S.A., 2016
Ley Lines, gradient books, Finland, 2016
some more strange meteorites, Meritage Press & i.e. Press, California & New York, U.S.A., 2017
the veil drops, Locofo Chaps, Chicago, U.S.A., 2017
a few geographies, White Knuckle Press, Birmingham, Alabama, U.S.A., 2017
The Waitstaff of Mar-a-Largo, Locofo Chaps, Chicago, U.S.A., 2017
bricolage, gradient books, Finland, 2017
random salamanders, A Wanton Text Production, Alexandria, Virginia, U.S.A., 2017
Circus economies, gradient books, Finland, 2017
The Word Factory: a miscellany, gradient books, Finland, 2018
The perfume of the abyss, Moria Books, Chicago, U.S.A., 2019
A vicarious life — the backing tracks, otata's bookshelf, Charleston, Illinois, 2019
taxonomic drift, Luna Bisonte Prods, Columbus, Ohio, U.S.A., 2019
Residual sonnets, ma press, Finland, 2019
Old Rhumba, gradient press, Finland, 2019
Art Informel, gradient press, Finland, 2019
turning to drones, Concrete Mist Press, Pennsylvania, U.S.A. 2020
turpentine, Luna Bisonte Prods, Columbus, Ohio, U.S.A., 2020
from *1750 Words*, SOd Press, Sydney, Australia, 2021
The Toast, Luna Bisonte Prods, Columbus, Ohio, U.S.A., 2021
The Sasquatch Walks Among Us, Sandy Press, Santa Barbara, California, U.S.A., 2021

Visual Poetry

Arachnid Nebula, Luna Bisonte Prods, Columbus, U.S.A., 2014
les échiquiers effrontés, Luna Bisonte Prods, Columbus, Ohio, U.S.A., 2018
The Comedians, SOd Press, Sydney, Australia, 2019

Art History

New Zealand Painting, 1950-1967, A.H. & A.W. Reed, Wellington, N.Z., 1968

Speculative Fiction

the allegrezza ficcione, Otoliths, Rockhampton, Australia, 2006

Memoir

sorties, Sandy Press, Santa Barbara, California, U.S.A., 2021

as co-editor with Jean Vengua

The First Hay(na)ku Anthology, Meritage Press, California, U.S.A., 2005
The Hay(na)ku Anthology, Vol. II, Meritage Press, California, U.S.A., 2008

www.ingramcontent.com/pod-product-compliance
Lightning Source LLC
Chambersburg PA
CBHW052048230426
43671CB00011B/1825
* 9 7 8 1 7 3 6 8 1 6 0 4 2 *